BLUEPRINT FOR WRITING

BLUEPRINT FOR WRITING

A WRITER'S GUIDE TO CREATIVITY CRAFT & CAREER

RACHEL FRIEDMAN BALLON

LOWELL HOUSE
Los Angeles

CONTEMPORARY BOOKS
Chicago

Ballon, Rachel Friedman.
    Blueprint for writing: a writer's guide to creativity, craft & career / Rachel
Friedman Ballon.
        p. cm.
    Includes bibliographical references and index.
    ISBN 1-56565-125-1
    1. Authorship. I. Title
PN151.B32 1994
808'.02--dc20   93-45926
                                                                     CIP

Lowell House
2029 Century Park East, Suite 3290
Los Angeles, CA 90067

Publisher: Jack Artenstein
Vice-President/Editor-in-Chief: Janice Gallagher
Director of Publishing Services: Mary D. Aarons
Project Editor: Bud Sperry
Text Design: Lisa-Theresa Lenthall
Typesetting: Tim Slavin

Manufactured in the United States of America
10 9 8 7 6 5 4 3 2 1

*Dedicated to those special men and women who helped me along
the path of this book. They know who they are.
Thank you!*

ACKNOWLEDGEMENTS

Writing a book is a collaborative effort, just like making a movie. This book evolved over the past decade and many people played a role in its development. To this end I'd like to thank the thousands of writing students who attended my workshops and taught me so much. Thank you to my private writing clients who were courageous enough to share their inner beauty and talent with me through their writing and their stories. A special thanks to a special group of women writers who have been in my private workshop for years—to my dear friend, Martine Greber Ehrenclou, Estrellita Mendez, Donna Daves Kent, and Jackeen Churchill. I'd like to thank everyone in the Writer's Program at UCLA, Ext. for allowing me to create so many different writing classes. Thanks to Beth Taylor, Head of American Film Institute Continuing Education, for her enthusiasm and support for my seminars and to her staff—Jan, Chris, and David for their help. I want to thank Kerry and Leah Cox for giving me the opportunity to be a columnist in Hollywood Scriptwriter Newsletter. *Many of my columns became the blueprint for chapters in this book. Thanks to Meera and Steve Lester and all their staff at the Writer's Connection, for inviting me to be a presenter at their yearly "Selling to Hollywood" conference. A thank you to all the staff at the Writer's Computer Store, especially Gabriele Zinke, Dan and Jesse Douma, and Patti, Linda, and Hugh who always answered questions when I needed computer assistance. A debt of gratitude to Marjorie Miller and Len Felder, my colleagues, for their valuable insights into the writing business and for their friendship.*

A warm thank you to Adrienne Fayne, my collaborator on the screenplay "Hit or Miss," for her loving friendship and to Steve Fayne for his generous legal expertise and counsel.

To my Editor at Lowell House, Bud Sperry, who believed that this book could be more than I thought and insisted on nothing less, for this I thank you. And thanks to Janice Gallagher, Editor-in-Chief, whose enthusiasm and support motivated me.

And lastly, I'd like to give a special thanks to my family, especially to my sons, Marc and John, who were always willing to read excerpts of the manscript and offered helpful suggestions throughout the writing of this book.

C O N T E N T S

> *"The inner shape of a man's life is what he writes from and about."*
>
> —Ross MacDonald

BLUEPRINT FOR WRITING IS DESIGNED FOR BEGINNING SCRIPT-writers, fiction writers, and professional writers who want a blueprint to follow when they write their scripts and manuscripts.

If you complete the *Blueprint for Writing* exercises at the end of each chapter, this book will enable you to master the craft of structuring a story for television movies, motion pictures, short stories, sitcoms, and novels. You will learn how to take your original idea and apply the lessons of this workbook until you have a completed script or manuscript. These finished works will showcase your writing ability and illustrate that you know how to structure your writing and develop memorable characters.

Just as an architect first creates a blueprint before constructing a building, a writer needs to create a blueprint before constructing his or her work. A blueprint keeps you headed in the right direction, gives structure to your story, and allows you to master the step-by-step techniques necessary for writing a successful script or novel.

I know many of you have tried to write a feature film, television movie, or book and failed. Some of you got bogged down in the middle, others had trouble finding the right direction to follow, but most of you just got stuck and quit, because you didn't know where to go, how to get there, and what to do next. These problems stopped you because you didn't have a plan or a *Blueprint for Writing* to follow.

This book will be your guide and show you how to develop the right plan or structure even *before* you begin writing your screenplay, teleplay, or novel. Your well-structured script or manuscript will not be written by accident or chance, but through the knowledge and skill you'll acquire from this book.

In 1980 I began teaching writing workshops at UCLA Extension in the Writer's Program. During the past decade I have taught thousands of writers—scriptwriters, fiction writers, children's writers, novelists, nonfiction writers, and playwrights. I also taught scriptwriting at the American Film Institute and from 1990–1993, I was an adjunct professor teaching characterization to film students in the School of Cinema and Television at USC Film School.

These writing workshops were always well attended. It was not surprising to me that so many people wanted to learn the craft of writing. The television, publishing, and film industries afford writers great financial rewards that few other industries offer. Where else can an unknown writer break in at the top by selling a million-dollar script or best-selling novel?

All it takes to make you an overnight success is that one fabulous, exciting script or manuscript! Sound easy? It isn't! Like all overnight successes you must first pay your dues by learning plot, dialogue, and mastering the craft of story, with an emphasis on structure and character development.

Originally, I wrote this book for the thousands of writing students taking my workshops and classes to use as a helpful resource to their writing. I also used *Blueprint for Writing* as the text for my scriptwriting classes at USC Film School and other institutions.

However, through word of mouth, knowledge of my book spread as I led workshops throughout the United States and Canada based on the material in *Blueprint for Writing*. The participants were delighted to have a step-by-step plan or "blueprint" to follow, guiding them from their original concept to completed script or manuscript.

After many years teaching writers, my intention in this book is to teach other writers how to "demystify" the writing process. I also want to give writers the tools for developing a "blueprint" to follow every time they start a new project.

Many students who attend my workshops are already working in the industry. Some are published writers, producers, assistant directors, readers, development executives, actors, and editors. Why are all these people taking writing courses in structure and character development if they are already in the business? Surprisingly, many of them don't know how to *structure* a script or novel and want to learn the basics of what it takes to create a great story and develop realistic and memorable characters.

After following the principles in *Blueprint for Writing* many of my students have sold scripts, others have had novels published.

Some have gotten staff positions on situation comedies and hour episodic dramas for television. Others have received writing assignments from production companies and networks after their scripts were read by story editors and producers who could tell these writers knew the craft of writing. And there were even a few who were awarded large advances for their as-yet-unwritten scripts or unpublished manuscripts.

Why did they receive assignments and advances for unfinished works? They were recognized and rewarded for their writing ability because the editors or producers realized they understood the basic techniques of writing. They also demonstrated a knowledge of how to develop interesting, complex characters. These entertainment and publishing industry executives were willing to risk money on these writers because they had proved themselves capable of laying out a plot structure and creating credible characters.

If you want to be a successful writer it doesn't matter whether you have prior writing experience. What does matter is your willingness to learn the fundamentals of writing and to work hard developing your craft.

Those who succeed as writers never give up. They write and rewrite and rewrite. They have the most important ingredient for writing success—perseverance and a strong desire to become writers. They can call themselves "writers" because they have mastered their craft, not because they just want to be known as "Writers!"

This book is for those of you who don't happen to live in Hollywood or New York City, where so many classes in scriptwriting and writing are taught. It is for you who live in Bellefonte, Pennsylvania, or Duluth, Minnesota, or Palm Beach,

Florida, and want to learn an easy-to-follow method of writing. A method that will work for you again and again.

When I first began writing this book it was strictly for scriptwriters, whose biggest problems always seemed to be structure and character development. But after I started teaching novelists, children's writers, playwrights, nonfiction writers, and short story writers in my "Creating Characters" workshop, I discovered fiction writers suffered from the same problems with structure and characterization as scriptwriters. Although the form of these two modes of writing is different, the process of structuring a novel and developing characters is similar.

From my teaching and consulting experience I have developed the *Balloncing* Method, a successful technique that demonstrates the necessary balance between CREATIVITY, CRAFT, and CAREER. Each component is related to the other, not treated as a separate entity but combined into a powerful whole. To become a successful writer takes the melding of each of these three diverse but equal and essential elements: free-flowing CREATIVITY, a command of your CRAFT, and the ability to market your writing CAREER. Writers who want a successful career need to perfect all three elements in order to sell their work.

In *Blueprint for Writing*, the first element you'll learn is how to tap into your most powerful resource—the unconscious—to increase creativity and discover ideas. The second step shows you how to take ideas and craft them into a plot structure. You'll learn how to create three-dimensional characters by taking your personal life stories and turning them into powerful, salable writing.

The last component will teach you how to survive and thrive in the current writer's marketplace. You'll learn how to present ideas with confidence and enthusiasm, to network and market your writing from the inside out. This includes learning techniques for overcoming writer's block, procrastination, and fear of rejection—the main roadblocks to your success.

By working *Blueprint for Writing*, you will have a step-by-step plan to guide you every inch of the way—from getting started to marketing your writing. By completing all the exercises at the end of each chapter you'll develop your own blueprint as well as a solid structure for your characters.

Make this book your creative tool and work with it! When you do, you'll be developing your ability and your improved results will become just the calling card you need to open doors for you! Then you'll be able to call yourself what I know each and every one of you can be: A writer!

UNLOCK YOUR CREATIVITY

"Ideas we don't know we have, have us."

—James Hill

IN THIS CHAPTER I'LL BE ADDRESSING THE FIRST ELEMENT OF THE *Ballon*cing method—Creativity. Creativity is free-flowing ENERGY and writing from this place creates free-flowing writing. Creativity has to be available to you at the beginning of your writing because without creative ideas, concepts, or thoughts you have nothing to write about and you can't start ANY writing project.

Creativity is where all poetry, art, drama, music, and ideas come from that touch people on a deep emotional level. Creativity is made up of two parts. First there is *Primary Creativity*, which comes from your unconscious and is the source of all new ideas and insights. It's where your inspiration comes from and makes up only 10 percent of the creative process. Then, there is *Secondary Creativity*, which is the 90 percent that involves editing, discipline, logic, structure, and order.

Creativity includes both inspiration and perspiration, and as a writer you need to discover how to combine the elements of ART or primary creativity that come from the right hemisphere of your brain with the elements of CRAFT or secondary creativity that comes from the left hemisphere of your brain. Both components are necessary to be a fully creative writer and you need to strike a balance between the two. For example, if an automobile is to run smoothly, all the parts must work together. If the engine breaks down, a tire goes flat, or you run out of gas, your car won't run. Each part depends upon the other.

The same holds true for writing. If you can access your creativity and come up with more ideas than you know what to do with, but you don't know how to put them into a craft or a structure, your writing will "break down," too. If you know craft, but have blocked your creativity, your writing will be flat and your characters will be weak and run out of gas. And finally, if you've mastered both craft and creativity, but don't know how to market yourself or your writing, you won't sell your work and your career will stall.

While developing my writing method, I recognized that each aspect of this writing process is similar to and can be compared with the different parts of any individual. Each person has a private self where all feeling, thinking, and imagination reside, and a public self that carries our observable behavior. Many times these different selves are in conflict. You might behave a completely different way from the way you're feeling inside. To be both a complete person and writer you need to integrate the sum of these parts into a whole. As a line of the song "Love and Marriage" goes, "You can't have one without the other."

As with individuals, different aspects of the writing process can conflict. Writers have to be both aware of their rich inner world and to have knowledge of and respect for the craft necessary to transform their shapeless inner world into a concrete form through mastery with words, thus adding new dimensions to the writer and to the writing.

To be more creative means to have the courage to return to childhood memories where you were freer and less self-conscious than you probably are now, and to allow that spontaneous creative side of you to emerge through your writing.

Abraham H. Maslow, author of the *Farther Reaches of the Human Nature*, said in an October 1962 lecture:

> *"The creative attitude requires both courage and strength and most studies of creative people have reported one or another version of courage ... that becoming more courageous makes it easier to let oneself be attracted by mystery, by the unfamiliar ... by the ambiguous and contradictory, by the universal and unexpected ...."*

In childhood, the fusion of primary and secondary creativity is found in all of us, but unfortunately is lost in most of us as we grow up and learn to hide our true self behind the many masks we wear. To become more creative is to allow yourself the opportunity to become a playful, joyous child, to be courageous and not afraid to let go, and have fun with your writing. By allowing your child to come out and play when you first begin to write, you'll be less judgmental, constricted, and rigid about your writing, and hopefully, the words will flow.

I have worked with many writers who were too into the results of their writing before they ever had anything written. This attitude stopped them and their creativity before they ever got started. You mustn't stop yourself with criticisms and judgments before you get your ideas down. If you do, you will stop yourself too soon in the process and not finish. It's important to suspend your judgment until AFTER you've written down your ideas, your story, or your concept. Otherwise, you will not be able to start your writing project, let alone finish it.

When you first begin to write, I want you to write by concentrating only on the writing process itself, not on the technique. Write down your ideas without worrying whether they're good enough. By writing in the moment you'll lose your past and future and your creativity will flow. This way of writing from your heart is the first burst of creative imagination that comes to you in a moment of insight or inspiration.

Haven't you ever started to write and when you looked at the clock hours had gone by when you thought you had only been working for minutes? You were being in the moment, totally immersed and absorbed in the present. You were involved in the process of writing, rather than in the product or results.

To be a productive and successful writer you must write from both your heart and your head, the basis of all great writing. This type of writing enables you to increase your creative output and allows you to reveal who you truly are and put it in your writing. When you write from your heart the writing is passionate, original, and honest and has great intensity and depth. To be a fully creative writer you must be open to all aspects of yourself, since repression of your feelings works against your creativity. If you avoid looking inside yourself, you'll lose parts of yourself and your experiences and you won't be able or willing to put those fertile ideas into your writing.

One excellent way for reconnecting with your inner self is to write in a journal. I tell both writing students and therapy clients to start a journal. Don't make it one of those fancy ones or one of those expensive handmade books. Buy a simple notebook, preferably one you can carry around with you at all times. It is a wonderful tool for helping you monitor what you're thinking, feeling, and dreaming about throughout the day and night. Get into the habit of writing in your journal every day. Record your thoughts, feelings, ideas, and even your dreams (both the day and the night ones).

Some people I work with have many different journals for specific things. One woman has a dream journal and a daily journal and a journal for childhood stories. I wholly recommend journals for nonwriters, too. They are a wonderful bridge between your external and internal selves. The only caution: don't write in your journal only when you're feeling depressed. Many people use a journal to dump their feelings and it gets to be a bad habit. To counteract that I tell people to buy a journal and call it their "Joyful Journal," and to write in it only those things that make them feel good.

Another type of journal you might try is a writer's journal where you can make different headings and sections according to dialogue, plot ideas, characters, and atmosphere. Keep this journal with you and you'll be surprised how much more observant you'll become of people, places, and things throughout your day. Writers need to be good observers of human behavior. What better way to heighten your ability to record human nature than to write in your journal. You'll be pleasantly surprised how many ideas you'll get for your future writing just from being more aware of your surroundings and the people in them. You'll see how much material you'll get at work, from friends, family, and in your personal relationships.

A young woman who was working on her masters in creative writing asked me to be her faculty advisor for the part of her curriculum that had to do with writing and dreams. I gave her assignments to record her dreams in her dream journal and then read them to me. From recording her dreams she got an idea to use one of her dreams as the basis for her master's thesis.

She is almost finished with her novel and I'm certain she would never have achieved that without first having her dream journal and making the commitment to use it.

Another client, a graduate film student, worked with me on her dreams because she felt her writing was shallow. One day she brought in a particular dream and we discussed it and how it related to her childhood. She took the germ of her dream and made a film from it, which she recently completed to wonderful reviews. The film emerged from her passion, her childhood, her truth, and from her dream. She wrote about something that came from the inside out and was meaningful to her, and that's why it stands out from other films, because it's personal.

I have consulted with experienced professionals who have had films produced, yet when starting a new project become blocked and are unable to write, because they're often afraid to connect to their inner worlds. Although they know craft, they avoid tapping their inner feelings and resist getting in touch with their emotions. Their writing remains stilted, their characters clichéd, and they don't sell their work until they're willing to express themselves without fear and reveal who they are.

To enable you to reach your inner depths, I will lead you in a writing exercise. You will begin the journey to travel beneath your mask and mine your childhood stories, memories, and emotions by using visualization and writing.

Visualization is the technique of imagining pictures. It closes off the left hemisphere of your brain and lets the right express insights and inspirations without criticisms. Visualization also involves the exploration of pictures that come to your mind, allowing you to experience a kind of waking dream.

First you need to get comfortable, close your eyes, and begin to breathe deeply. Continue breathing until you feel the muscles in your body relax completely. After you are relaxed, visualize yourself as a small child. Picture yourself in a natural setting such as a meadow, a park, the woods, or by the ocean. As you visualize, be part of the scene with all your senses. Smell the sea air, listen to the birds singing, hear the wind rustling through the leaves, and see the myriad colors of the ocean. Really get into the scene and imagine yourself to be there completely. What are you wearing? How does your hair look? What expression do you have on your face? Are you alone or with a friend? Take a few more moments and visualize what you're feeling in this wonderful childhood place. Are you happy? Sad? Lonely? Playful? Free?

Now take your pen and start writing about the experience. Using first person (I), present tense (am), write with all your senses, describing the visual pictures you experienced. Do not stop writing until you've written for twenty minutes or more. Do not take your pen from the page and don't read over anything you've written until you're finished.

If you get stuck and can't think of anything else to write, then write about feeling stuck and not being able to write. No matter what—don't stop writing until at least twenty minutes have passed. If you want, you could set a timer and not stop until it goes off.

Writing about this waking dream *without* any type of structure or rules enables you to powerfully access dramatic stories and memories from your past. This type of writing is known as free or automatic writing, and combined with visualization, offers a direct path to the unconscious and to your buried treasures—emotions, feelings, memories.

In my WRITING FROM THE HEART–WRITING FROM THE HEAD workshops, I spend the first day showing writers how to tap into their inner world by doing these specific writing exercises. By going on this visual journey, many writers come up with extraordinary images they then record through the written word, describing all the details through their sense of smell, sight, sound, taste, and touch.

Next, they take their childhood memories and stories and transform them into fictional characters and plots. Many writers were surprised at both the quality and power of this writing. Others never approached writing from the perspective of including *both* creativity and craft at the same time and found this technique allowed them to write with greater ease and intensity.

After you've completed writing about your childhood memory, see if you can put it into a story or scene. My main objective for having you write this way is to get you to write *your* TRUTH, to write *your* PASSION by taking your memories and transforming them into well-structured, salable stories that move others emotionally. When you write from this powerful source you will be able to create fresh stories and original characters who come alive.

A tool for self-knowledge and self-discovery, free writing allows you to self-explore your unconscious. Not only will your writing improve, but writing your childhood stories will put you on the path of healing. Dealing with your past through writing will also make you feel better and relieve stress.

Remember, when you begin to write you just want to get your creative ideas down on the page without the self-consciousness of your judgmental self. When you analyze and criticize your writing too soon in the writing process you may become blocked. So silence your critic by continuing to write without editing your work, no matter what! When you first get it down, don't worry about grammar, spelling, or punctuation. This free writing must be done without self-criticism. There is certainly plenty of time for that.

Just write without censoring your thoughts, feelings, or ideas before you ever ask yourself: "Is it good?" "Does it work?"

The only thing you should be concerned with at the beginning of your writing journey is to get your words down on the page. Just get out of the way of your creative self and trust the process.

Successful writers have an openness to themselves and their writing. Trust that process and you will end up rich with imagination, spontaneity, and creativity, all the ingredients you need for writing success. When you are able to write from the inside out, your writing improves.

I always tell writers when they first begin a project: "It doesn't have to be right, just WRITE it!"

Creativity must be nurtured. It is one of the real gifts in life that is also free for the taking. It's up to you to untie the bow and open your gift each and every day!

BLUEPRINT FOR WRITING

1. Start the day with a new approach. Instead of writing on your computer try a legal pad with pen because you will write more naturally without worrying about a mechanical process. Get a change of scenery. Don't write at your desk, go out in nature and relax.

2. Put on relaxing music when you write and put the rhythms of the music into the rhythms of your words.

3. Trust your "gut feelings" and your natural instincts. When you first start to write learn to rely more on your intuition than your logic.

4. Take a break from your writing and go for a walk on your favorite path. Take time to discover new things you've never seen before—pretend you're a tourist.

5. Take five to fifteen minutes a day to daydream. Really allow your imagination to soar and let your playful child come out, then write from your child's voice.

6. Read poetry for at least ten minutes before you begin to write. Nursery rhymes are especially good, because they have a natural rhythm and meter, which can connect you to your creativity.

7. Visit the ocean, a river, or park and write a brief paragraph about your experience. Describe the colors, sounds, and smells of nature in words using your sense of touch, taste, sound, sight, and smell.

8. Set a timer for at least twenty to thirty minutes when you first start to write. Don't stop writing until the timer goes off. This automatic writing will help you avoid being critical or judgmental.

9. Start a journal and write in it daily. Record your feelings and thoughts as well as noting human behavior and relationships. This will sharpen your observation skills.

10. Start a dream journal and record your daydreams as well as your night dreams. Your dreams will provide you with a wealth of material for your writing projects. Listen to your dreams—you created them!

HOW DOES SCRIPTWRITING DIFFER FROM FICTION WRITING?

"Every style that is not boring is a good one."
—Voltaire

LET'S DISCUSS SOME OF THE DIFFERENCES BETWEEN SCRIPTWRITING and fiction writing. The format of scriptwriting is completely different from fiction writing. Scriptwriting is a craft unto itself, with a special format, specific margins, and a highly developed structure.

However, the same rules of structure and character development apply to a well-written novel as to a script. I included fiction writers because I recognized they needed help with structure and characterization just as much as scriptwriters.

Unfortunately, many fiction writers begin their work without having any idea where they are going. Perhaps they only know the opening sentence. In fact, some fiction writers never use an outline or plan to work from. As some writers have stated, they just let their characters take them where they want to go. Do you know where they usually end up? Stuck at a dead end. Whether you're writing a script or a novel you should always have an outline first. Without one, writing is a disaster. This happened to a beginning novelist who consulted with me on her first novel. She had taken a class where the teacher said, "Let the characters talk to you and take you where they want to go."

By the time the poor woman came to me she had written well over six hundred pages and guess where her characters took her—to a dead end! She had no story, no structure, and excessive plots all leading nowhere. After she told me her story, without even reading it I told her she had two novels going on simultaneously and that's why she had six hundred pages without a resolution.

My suggestion was to start over and create an outline. If she had done that in the first place, she would have saved a lot of time, trouble, and confusion. But all's well that ends well and she worked for a couple of more years from a well-detailed outline and now has a well-crafted, best-selling novel.

Since consulting with professional writers, I've discovered that successful fiction writers almost always work from a detailed outline. Recently, a lawyer who retired from his successful practice and wanted to become a novelist met with me. He resisted my telling him he must outline his novel before he began writing. He began to write without an outline and after a couple of months was hopelessly lost in the maze of his work. He called me in a panic, and this time he followed my advice about outlining his work BEFORE he actually began to write the novel. He spent a lot of time working on his outline and ended up with a twenty-five page, detailed chapter-by-chapter outline. From that point his writing was a breeze, because of the time and effort he spent to lay out the story. When he actually started writing his novel he could concentrate on developing in-depth characters and build suspense in his plot. He was able to write his novel with ease and he finished it much sooner than he would have if he had not used an outline. He's now working on his second novel—busy doing the outline *first*.

There are major differences between fiction writing and scriptwriting. In scriptwriting you always tell your story through the main character's point-of-view. When writing a novel you can change point-of-view from one character to another, although you still need to focus on and tell a specific main character's story.

Another difference is that in fiction writing you may have as many pages as you want to complete your work. You can divide your book into chapters, sections, or parts as you write. You may have as few as one hundred pages or as many as a thousand. You can begin with one character's story and change to another's on the same page. You can go back and forth in time, from present to past to future in the same chapter. You can devote pages just to describing the scenery, the setting, or the characters. You can take chapters to reveal your characters' inner thoughts and feelings, writing stream of consciousness and playing God.

That is not the case with scriptwriting. In a script you can't go into your character's head and tell what your characters think or feel. You can only show what they do in action and say in dialogue. In no way may the author intrude his or her thoughts into the story.

Whatever amount of time the script covers, that is the amount of time it takes the audience to view it. When you write a script, you don't have time to wander about like you do in a novel. During a feature film or television movie-of-the-week you only have a limited amount of time to tell your story, usually ninety minutes to two hours, with few exceptions. You can see why it is so important to tell your story and get to your destination (the end) as quickly as possible. When writing a novel you may go in any direction you want, taking side trips along the way, and zigzagging back and forth from beginning to end. When you begin a script you must always know the ENDING first! Before you write a single word you must know the final destination.

A novel will be read by an individual who can put the book down whenever he or she chooses, for an hour, a day, a week, or a year, and pick it up whenever he wants to. It doesn't matter how long in terms of time it takes to read the book. She can start in the beginning and skip to the end, go back to the beginning, turn to the middle. He can read every word or just scan it. But in a script you can't take your time, you must tell your story fast and get to the resolution as quickly as possible.

A script is a narrative that tells a story through the use of moving pictures with forward-moving linear action. It goes in a direct line from beginning to end. Fiction writers must also be able to write a story with a beginning, a middle, and an end. This is "the structure" and without it you have nothing.

The structure is your plot line and in a script there are usually one or more subplots besides the main story. They are secondary to the main plot and if they are well-written, at the end they will connect to the main plot. In a novel you may have many subplots going at the same time and they, too, should be tied to the main storyline.

Many people resist learning dramatic structure. They always manage to find those few exceptions to the rule of movies or novels that have been successful without being tightly structured. That is all well and good. But first you must learn the rules before you can break them. If you want to become a successful writer you must master the rules and techniques of classical structure, a structure that has its origins in ancient Greece.

The Greek classics were written by famous playwrights such as Sophocles, Euripides, Aristophanes, and Aeschylus, to name a few. They stressed structure and many of our contemporary playwrights based their successful plays on the principles laid down by the Greek dramatists. Eugene O'Neill, Tennessee Williams, and Arthur Miller were greatly influenced by these writers.

In Aristotle's "Poetics," he states, "...some plots are simple while others are complex. By complex I mean action in which change arises with either recognition or reversal or both. These ought to arise from the construction of the plot itself...." He continues later, "It is apparent, therefore, that the solutions of plots ought to happen as a result of the plots themselves and not from a contrivance...."

In today's terminology that means each scene should cause the scene that follows it and evolve from the scene that preceded it. Events in a script must arise from cause-and-effect writing and must not be contrived or happen by accident. You can't have the Greek chorus solving the problem. It has to be motivated within the story and characters.

This is known as *causal* writing. You lay out all the scenes so they are connected to one another. Think of all the scenes as pieces of a giant jigsaw puzzle. You try to connect all of them so you can see the entire picture. That also applies to fiction writers. Every chapter is also a part of a puzzle and must be a part of the overall picture. The novel, although not as highly structured as a script, must have cause-and-effect writing, too. The biggest writing problems I've seen both with beginners and professional writers is that their scripts or novels are episodic, not written in a causal manner. That means the scenes or chapters don't lead to the next one. There's no blueprint that holds the structure together and the scenes occur without connection or purpose.

Remember when you were a small child you'd beg your parents to read you a bedtime story? The most exciting stories were always those that usually started, "Once upon a time ...." It could be a story about "Cinderella," her wicked stepsisters, stepmother, the glass slipper, and the handsome prince. It could be the story of "Snow White and the Seven Dwarfs," and how the seven dwarfs saved her from the wicked queen. Some stories were about animals such as "The Three Pigs," or "Little Red Riding Hood and the Big Bad Wolf." Whether the stories were about beautiful young princesses, princes, witches, or animals they held your interest from the "Once upon a time ..." to "...they lived happily ever after."

You listened enthralled and wanted to know, "What's going to happen next?" No matter how many times you heard the stories you were never bored, even when you knew the ending. Why? Because you were emotionally involved in the conflict of the hero. You rooted for the hero or heroine and hoped someone would save him or her from the bad guy, who was a threat. This created conflict and suspense and you felt afraid for them. You felt relieved when someone was saved in the end, usually by the hero or heroine.

The one thing these stories all had in common was STRUCTURE. They had a beginning, a middle, and an end. You felt satisfied when the bad guy lost, and the hero or heroine won. The conflict began immediately and the story ended when the conflict was resolved.

These stories will last forever. They have all the necessary building blocks needed to construct any good story, and you will use these same building blocks when you construct your story. You'll probably read them to your children and your grandchildren. Now, read them for yourself to see what the necessary elements are for telling a good story.

There are many other differences between scriptwriting and fiction writing. For example, in scriptwriting you always tell your story through your main character's point-of-view. And scriptwriting always has a limited point-of-view. However, in fiction writing you can use different points-of-view.

Even though you've just read about the differences in scriptwriting and fiction writing there are some exceptions to the rule. As a fiction writer you're writing for the "I want it now," generation, which doesn't want to spend a lot of time on extraneous details. They are used to television, McDonalds, and ATM machines and not used to waiting.

Today, most novels are no longer filled with long descriptions that go on for page after page like the novels of the past. Readers like the stage to be set and to see the action unfold in the present, as if viewing an action scene on television and in the movies. They don't want the author to tell them what's happening, they like the action to unfold on the page. So, put your scene on stage and let the characters play it out before your reader's eyes. SHOW AND DON'T TELL is the caveat for the modern fiction writer.

BLUEPRINT FOR WRITING

1. Read fairy tales to learn what makes a good story. What elements in fairy tales are used to tell a good story?

2. Create your own fairy tale using all the elements in regular fairy tales. Be sure you have a beginning, middle, and end.

3. Read the Greek tragedies to study structure. *Oedipus Rex* by Sophocles is a wonderful example of the unities of time, place, and action.

4. Get a book on Greek myths such as Edith Hamilton's *Mythology* or Joseph Campbell's *Hero With a Thousand Faces*, and study them for dramatic structure.

5. Try to put your story into the structure of a Greek myth. Were you able to do it?

6. Whose point-of-view are you writing from in your script? Do you tell your story from the main character's point-of-view?

7. What does episodic writing mean? Is your writing episodic? Change your writing so it's connected scene by scene.

SELECTING YOUR STORY

"I write entirely to find out what I am thinking,
what I want, and what I fear."
—JOAN DIDION

THE WRITER IS NOT ONLY THE CREATOR OF THE SCRIPT, BUT HER choice of material will either make the experience an exciting adventure or an agonizing voyage.

Although this chapter doesn't concern itself with the actual techniques of writing, it does deal with the most important element in the writing process—YOU, the writer.

As a psychotherapist, I feel it's very important to include this chapter for many pertinent reasons. Before you begin your writing journey it's necessary for you to answer the following questions:

- DO YOU KNOW WHY YOU WANT TO WRITE?
- DO YOU WANT TO MAKE A LOT OF MONEY?
- DO YOU WANT TO BE FAMOUS?
- DO YOU WANT TO GET RECOGNITION?

- DO YOU WANT TO ENTERTAIN OTHERS?
- DO YOU WANT ONLY TO BE KNOWN AS A WRITER WITHOUT HAVING TO WRITE?

If these are your only reasons for wanting to become a writer give it up now, because they're all the wrong reasons. It's important to look at your motives for wanting to write, because if they aren't strong enough you probably won't finish what you start. Writing is just too difficult a craft to learn if you aren't serious about it.

But maybe you feel you have something important to say and want to share it with others. Perhaps you want to tell people about your strong feelings and beliefs through the written word. Or you have a burning desire to tell your personal story. If deep down inside you feel you must write, that you can't live without writing, then writing is for you.

The famous writer Rainer Maria Rilke gave the following advice to an aspiring writer in his book *Letters To A Young Poet*, "This above all—ask yourself in the stillest hour of your night: 'Must I write?' And if this should be affirmative, if you may meet this earnest question with a strong and simple 'I must,' then build your life according to this necessity: your life even into its most indifferent and slightest hour must be a sign of this urge and a testimony to it."

Do you feel the way Rilke described? If the answer for you is "I must," then keep writing.

In my writing classes I have students answer the question: "WHY I WRITE?" The following is an excerpt from this exercise by one of my writing students:

WHY I WRITE

"I write to stay sane. I write to claim my mind for me, to stop it from wandering off down the freeway leaving my body at the steering wheel of the car, driving downtown instead of exiting at Gower for physical therapy. If I see words on the page, forming off the end of my pencil, it makes sense out of what is going on inside and outside of my head. I write so I can cry over the page and not in front of people I meet. I write so that I can be brave, spirited, positive, and joyful for J. It is okay if I sometimes fail, which has happened a lot lately. I used to think I would write stories for pleasure, to entertain, to amuse, and yes, to say some things I want the folks back home to notice. Now I know that isn't true. Perhaps, it never was true. I write on the paper or in my head on and off day and night . . . Sometimes I yell, "Wahoo, Yellow Dogs." That's honest, really honest. Most of the time I write the words down because it feels so good. It comforts me. This morning I wrote one sentence and cried for fifteen minutes. It was hard to start writing again, so I wandered mindless around the house. When I picked up the pencil again, I was tired, but I felt better."

As you can see, writing is absolutely meaningful and necessary in this person's life. She is a talented writer who has just finished her first children's book about her life growing up in the south. It is a wonderful, delightful book that I know will sell, because it's personal yet professionally written.

As we discussed in the previous chapter, writing must be personal or it is not worth writing. Yet some writers have problems writing their personal story. Many times it is too painful for them to express inner emotions such as love, hate, fear, joy, sorrow, anger, or despair. These feelings are very private and some writers may be afraid of exposing themselves. But successful writers must reveal their true selves—who they are, what they feel, what they fear.

If you are unable to do this, you have already failed as a writer. No matter how exciting your story may be, if it doesn't have emotional content no one will care to see or read it. Your audience or reader wants to be able to relate to your characters, to identify with their problems, and to root for them.

You should take your time before choosing your story and give a lot of serious consideration to the selection of your subject matter. To capture your audience, you must touch them in an emotional way, all the more reason for you to be open and honest when you write. Above all, you should write what you know. Don't try to write a story about life in the merchant marine if you have no idea what that's like. However, if you have a burning desire to write about a subject you know nothing about and you're going to write it no matter what, then—DO THE NECESSARY RESEARCH BEFORE YOU START WRITING! If you don't, your story will fall apart because it won't ring true and nobody will want to read it.

Whatever you write put your passion, your values, and your beliefs into your story. It is always better to write about some personal experience you feel passionate about, but not so close you can't be objective. When you're personally involved you're emotionally involved, and your readers and viewers will also be involved with your story and characters.

On the other hand, there has to be a balance between being too personal or too professional. Some writers are so obsessed with structure and the external aspect of writing they always take writing classes and buy every writing book on the market, but they ignore their internal resources. Their writing becomes clichéd and their characters are one-dimensional and have no heart, because they concentrate only on craft and not on themselves as the creators of the work.

If you try to conceal who you are behind your characters, your script or manuscript will never work. To be a good writer you must have the courage to expose yourself and risk being vulnerable. I have had many talented students who were so close to their stories they were unwilling and unable to be objective. When they were given suggestions to improve their stories they refused to make the necessary changes.

"But that's how it really happened," they would argue when they received constructive criticism. These writers were too personally involved in the story to be able to see it with the necessary objectivity of the "writer's eye."

It doesn't matter if what you write about really happened. What is important is for you to take a personal story and make it dramatic and entertaining, and to put the truth of your "self" into it. You can only do that if you are able to care about your story, yet be objective enough to change it if it doesn't work.

Before I discuss the process of selecting your story, I want to caution you about what *not* to write. It is inevitable in every workshop that one student will ask, "How do I know what the networks or publishers are buying?"

"You don't know!" I exclaim.

"What's commercial this year?"

"Nobody knows," I reply.

To want to be commercial is not a good enough reason to write. By the time you write what you think will be a "hot subject" you'll already be too late. You can't outguess networks, publishers, and studios who have staffs on payroll just to read newspapers, magazines, and new books on the market. If you think I'm kidding, what about the Amy Fisher–Joey Buttafuoco affair? In a very short time all three networks plus a few cable stations came out with their movie-of-the-week version of the affair. And a production company had a script in the works about the Branch Davidian siege near Waco, Texas. The filming of the script was already in production and they only stopped because they had to wait to see the outcome of the real-life siege so they would know how to end the film version.

Can you recall all the books that came out almost immediately after a major newsworthy event or death of a celebrity? And now that we have so many reality talk shows and all those supermarket tabloids, there is NOTHING you'll be able to get that will scoop these organizations unless, of course, you do something sensational and then you'll probably sell your story to the highest bidder.

So you see why it doesn't pay to try to be commercial. You'll be wasting your time. But you'll always be commercial when you write something new, fresh, and original—something that comes from your life experience, from your heart. Then you'll at least have a chance of selling your writing, because it will be unique with you. It will then have a chance of becoming a commercial success because of your commitment to your story and your need to share what you have to say. You'll never sell the overdone, clichéd work you're so sure will be commercial. Do you know why? Because it's been done over and over again.

Assuming you have given up the notion of wanting to be commercial, let's examine how you select a story to write. I want to assure you that your choice doesn't happen by accident.

In my therapy practice, I deal with many individuals concerning their personal relationships and inner conflicts. When they are relating their problems and recalling painful memories, many therapy clients experience a release from strong emotions they had suppressed for years. After they dredge up these feelings in therapy and talk about them they often feel better and experience a lightness and a surge of new-found energy as they loosen the ties from the "ghosts of the past." They often have a sense of freedom and are better able to handle their present conflicts and relationships.

Yet, there are other individuals who suppress past experiences and continue to suffer in the present. They can't seem to remember any details of their past and end up feeling blocked and frustrated. When that occurs I use writing exercises as a method to help them release the pent-up emotions they're unable or unwilling to verbalize. In these cases where the person is blocked, I discovered that writing instead of talking was a highly effective therapeutic tool when clients were unable to recall their childhood. Through writing they were eventually able to release their blocks and to discover their repressed emotions.

I also noticed the same phenomenon would sometimes happen to certain writers in my workshops. When their script or manuscript involved a personal story dealing with some painful aspect of their past, their repressed feelings would manifest themselves in writer's block. With my help and guidance the writers would work through their creative or psychological blocks. I had them stop writing their script and start doing writing exercises. These exercises helped them work through their personal blocks and after doing them, they broke free from their blocks. The wonderful breakthroughs they made in their writing allowed them to experience many of the same positive benefits my therapy clients experienced.

To further illustrate this point let me relate a few actual examples. I've changed the names of those students involved to protect their privacy.

A woman in one of my workshops, whom I'll call Lydia, was writing a script about a successful career woman and her teen-age daughter. The mother was attractive while the daughter was plain and overweight. She was also unpopular in school and very unhappy with her mother. The two had a terrible relationship that kept getting worse. The daughter became more and more rebellious and the mother became more distant and involved in her work.

Lydia worked and worked on her story, but couldn't figure out the ending. She kept going around in circles. First, she'd make the mother the main character. Then she'd rewrite the ending and change it so the daughter would be the main character. She couldn't get to the core of her story and kept going off on tangents. Her story had no focus, no resolution, and it didn't work.

Every time a classmate would make a suggestion to her, Lydia would become angry and defensive. Rather then listen to helpful criticism, she would argue and become upset. After a long struggle, Lydia finally set up the story so the two women would have a confrontation in the climax. The daughter would confess she was secretly jealous of her mother and the mother would break down and reveal to her daughter that she had always felt inadequate as a mother and used her work as an escape from the relationship. In the end of the story, the daughter and mother discovered they really loved each other and the two arrived at a new understanding and a much better relationship.

The mother was finally able to express her love for her daughter. The daughter finally developed a loving attitude toward her mother and herself.

Lydia was like a new person after she finished her script. She lost her defensive attitude and was much happier. She later told the class that the characters were difficult for her to deal with because she discovered while writing the script they really were her mother and herself.

When she chose to write this story she wasn't consciously aware of that, but only after she began to get involved with the characters and their relationship did she realize they were really autobiographical. Through the process of writing the script, Lydia was able to let go of the deep feelings of anger she felt toward her own mother who was deceased. She eventually arrived at a new self-awareness about her mother and herself. Lydia was finally able to forgive her mother, and in the process, forgive herself. She began to release negative feelings from the past and turn them into positive ones. Writing the script was therapeutic for her.

From the above example you can see the need to be careful not to choose a story that is too personal, because it doesn't always work out to be as rewarding an experience as Lydia's. Remember, she didn't give up and kept on working until she got it right, no matter how frustrating the writing became or how many unpleasant feelings arose while she was writing her script.

Choosing the right subject can help you work through "unfinished business" or be a dress rehearsal to do those things you're afraid to do in your own life. However, when the wounds are too raw, writing about a personal experience can be like "rubbing salt in the wound."

A young man I'll call Bob wanted to write a script about a recently divorced man struggling to be on his own. The main character, married for 26 years, was trying to be independent and deal with all of the problems besetting a man living alone. He had to learn to cook, clean, and develop a new social life, while still experiencing the painful feelings of divorce.

Bob had a lot of problems trying to write his story and he couldn't get a solid handle on it. I spoke with him and soon discovered he was too close to the story, because he was actually going through a divorce himself. Every time he'd write a particular scene he'd begin to relive his pain all over again. Since he wasn't detached and couldn't get enough distance to look at his script objectively, he couldn't write it. In reality, Bob was writing his actual life story as he was living it and this didn't make for either dramatic writing or healthy living.

When other students began to give him suggestions he would respond defensively "Well, that's the way it really happened." He was too emotionally involved with his own real-life drama to maintain the distance he needed from his work.

I finally persuaded Bob to put his script aside for the time being and write about something else that wasn't as emotionally upsetting. Eventually, he chose another story that wasn't as personal. He enjoyed writing it so much that it helped him forget a lot of his own pain.

With his new story Bob was finally able to become objective and listen to advice as he worked on his script. He wasn't defensive and made changes without getting angry. I began to notice a real change in Bob's personality as he worked on the new script. He became less depressed and more optimistic about his future. I know someday Bob will probably go back and write his original story about his divorce. It could make a good script, but not until he is emotionally able to write it and still remain dispassionate.

Bob certainly isn't the only writer I know who had to give up a story. There's really a fine balance between writing what you know and maintaining the proper emotional distance from your work. Each of you should strive to look at your work as a professional writer and choose material that has meaning for you and which you can change when you have to, without resistance.

Choosing to write a story you can live with can often help you work through some unresolved conflict in your life. When you begin to write your story you go on a journey at the same time your main character does. Resolving your story can sometimes lead to resolution of your own inner conflicts, becoming an experience of personal healing and growth.

That was the case for Janet, a beautiful young woman in one of my workshops. She began to write a novel about a famous actress with tremendous popularity, whose fan club was so huge she received thousands of letters and calls a week.

However, in the story one fan goes too far and begins to stalk her, eventually accosting the actress when she rejects him. She becomes terrified and so afraid to leave her house she becomes paranoid. Soon she is at the point of being unable to function in both her personal and professional life and feels she's falling apart emotionally.

In class, Janet kept getting stuck and couldn't seem to write the climax of her novel. Eventually, it came out during class discussion that she was identifying too closely with her main character. In reality, one night when Janet's car broke down on a deserted highway, a passerby came to her aid. Instead of helping her, he attacked her. She was stabbed and he attempted to rape her, but she got away.

This terrifying incident, which had happened years earlier, traumatized Janet. She was still frightened and suffered from anxiety attacks and nightmares. She felt violated and victimized to the point that it negatively affected her present relationships.

As she wrote each new chapter she began to work through her unresolved anger and her feelings of helplessness. Janet identified with her main character and had her do all of the things Janet was unable to do in real life. In the novel, her main character began to fight back against her attacker and in the climactic scene she stabs him in order to save herself.

Janet's openness with the class allowed her to begin to free pent-up fears she had suppressed for years following the attack. This freeing-up of unfinished business allowed her to become unblocked. She started to write her novel with new energy, because she had released her creative energy by writing through her fears in her novel.

Once she was finished, Janet had resolved her internal conflicts and her anxiety disappeared. She also felt in control of her life once again and by finishing her novel without giving up, she helped heal herself.

When you decide on the story you want to write, it is an absolute necessity for you to put yourself in the position of your audience, asking yourself, "Will they understand what I'm writing?" "Am I getting my point across?" "Am I being objective?" "Am I too emotionally involved?"

If you're only writing for yourself, forget about writing to sell, and write in a journal or a diary. No one is interested in your latest love affair or breakup. Write about them in your journal!

Your first goal as a professional writer is to entertain your audience. A professional writer takes her personal story and makes it dramatic. So put the script or novel about your divorce or latest love affair back in your drawer. Instead, write a story that will be a positive experience for you and one that will evoke strong emotional responses from your audience, who will identify with your characters and your honesty.

BLUEPRINT FOR WRITING

1. Which stories do you feel passionate about writing? Write about why you feel this way.

2. Write a couple of pages answering the question, "Why I Write?"

3. Can you be objective about your work? If you can't, write about why. Are you writing about something that just happened? Are you too close to the subject? Does it hurt when you write about it?

4. Do you care enough about your story to work on it for a year or more if it's a script or novel? If the answer is yes, why do you feel this way?

5. Why do you want to write this story? Do you want to share your beliefs with others? Do you have something philosophical to say? Do you have a moral or ethic you feel strongly about? Why?

6. What unfinished business do you want to resolve, if any? Are you angry about a past injustice? Do you want to get even for a wrong? Do you want to work through some childhood pain?

7. Is your story too personal for you to write? If so, why? Does it hurt too much? Is the problem or relationship too painful? Are you too emotionally invested to write it with the necessary professional distance?

8. What are your motives for writing this story? Write them down. Are they the right motives? Do you want to right a wrong? Do you want to make things happen in your story that you can't make happen in your life? Do you want to imagine the way things ought to be?

HOW DO YOU BEGIN?

"I always begin with a character, or characters, and then try to think up as much action for them as possible."

—JOHN IRVING

S HOULD I DEVELOP A CHARACTER FIRST AND THEN A STORY, OR should I develop a story first and then create a character?"

This is the question many beginning writers ask when they first start their projects.

My answer is: "You don't develop either one first or second. Story and character develop from each other." Because Character is Action and Action is Character. What does this mean? Let's see:

Do you remember that special relative you always loved and admired? Do you ever wonder about the mysterious couple who lived in your neighborhood and never left their home? Do you still fantasize about the most beautiful girl in your class, the one you had a crush on years ago?

In all of the above examples you had a particular person in mind, someone you knew, liked, or feared. If you decided to write about any one of those people you would end up with a character, but you wouldn't have a story. It would then be your job to take the character and put him or her in an exciting story. You would do that by getting to know your character so well that you'd begin to create the proper environment, problems, and conflicts for your character. Your story would develop as your character would. Character films and character books are those in which the character determines the action. Films such as *Tootsie*, *The Great Santini*, or *Rocky* are examples of character films. Books like *Gone With The Wind* or *Ordinary People* are character-oriented. You'd never create a frail, slight, educated character to play the role of Rocky. Nor would you get a stocky, muscle-bound man to play Tootsie. Would you ever choose a meek, unattractive character to portray Scarlett O'Hara?

Who your character is, what she thinks, feels, and believes will determine how she will behave. Your character's actions must be consistent with his personality. This will be discussed in more depth later in a chapter on characters.

On the other hand, let's suppose you have always been interested in subjects such as World War II, airplane crashes, or oceanography. These subjects have intrigued you, so you've decided you want to write a book or script featuring one of them. You'd then need to create a character who would relate to the subject you chose and who would motivate the proper action for your work.

Whether or not you choose a character for your subject or a subject for your character, you then must create a story that is exciting and dramatic for your structure. Some examples of subject-type films are: *The Dirty Dozen*, *Alive*, and *Jaws*.

Let's suppose you can't come up with an interesting subject or a fascinating character, what do you do? You must have some strong opinions and feelings about certain social issues confronting you in the world you live. They could be nuclear waste, criminal justice, or child abuse. These are a few examples of broad issues you could deal with that would interest your audience. But an issue alone is not enough. In each case you need to create a character and a story to dramatize your point of view about the issue. Movies like this include: *The China Syndrome*, *Silkwood*, and *Something About Amelia*. Books about issues are *To Kill A Mockingbird*, *The Color Purple*, and *This Boy's Life*.

It really doesn't matter how or where you get your idea for a manuscript or script. What does matter is that you care about what you write. For me, the most successful stories are those small personal ones about the average man or woman. Stories about people who want what you and I want, who feel what you and I feel are the ones everyone can identify with.

Emotional relationships between people make the most powerful stories. Stories that involve personal struggles have the most impact. Stories about lovers, families, friends, and enemies are universal and touch everyone. They deal with the powerful emotions of love, hate, joy, sorrow, anger, jealousy, and fear. This is the stuff from which great films and novels are created. Examples of these are *Ordinary People*, *Dead Poets Society*, and *The Joy Luck Club*. These works make you laugh and cry, but most of all they make you FEEL. They move you just the way they moved the person who wrote them. They were written by people who really cared and in turn, made the audience and reader really care.

As you think about your writing take the raw materials buried inside you and start to mine them. Discover the human element of your story and make it personal. By doing this your writing will become universal and everyone who sees or reads it will be emotionally involved.

BLUEPRINT FOR WRITING

1. Do you really care about this story, character, or issue?

2. Write about your burning desire, cause, or belief. What do you want to share with others?

3. Write about a person from your past who has influenced or impacted your life.

4. What special knowledge or experiences could you write about in a story?

5. Which story are you passionate about? Why?

CONSTRUCTING THE FRAMEWORK

"I don't see how anybody starts a movie without knowing how it's going to end."

—JOHN BARTH

B Y NOW YOU'VE CHOSEN THE CHARACTER, SUBJECT, OR ISSUE YOU want to write about. But you aren't certain what to do next. The next thing you do is NOTHING! That is, don't write down anything on paper. Live with your idea for a while. Think about it twenty-four hours a day. Let it germinate. Mull it over, sleep with it, think about it before you commit any words to paper.

It is important for you to look at all aspects of your idea. You need to explore all the different possibilities open to you. If you give your idea enough time to germinate, a story will eventually begin to appear. Thinking about your story will make it begin to take a shape. But to have your vague idea become a well-structured story, you must do more than think. You need to deal with the craft of structuring your story and that means organizing your time, thoughts, and ideas. It requires discipline to develop the proper structure you'll need so your writing won't collapse.

Let's compare writing to building a house. When you want to build a home, an architect first draws up a set of plans. A blueprint. He can't do that until you give him pertinent information about the style you prefer. Do you want a California ranch or an English Tudor? Maybe you want a two-story colonial complete with columns. Or do you prefer Spanish modern?

Whatever style you choose determines the blueprint. Your architect must know the *desired end result* before she draws up plans for your house. From the blueprints he will construct the framework that holds your house together. The framework is the skeleton of your home and without that your house would collapse.

The process is the same when you start to build your manuscript or script. You must first create your *Blueprint for Writing* before you begin writing. I guarantee it's easier to create an outline to follow as a guide or direction for your story than to write without one. Writers who resist developing an outline because they think it stops their creative flow or takes too much time and energy, eventually end up wasting their time and sapping all their energy, because they develop writer's block and after a few pages, don't know what to do or where to go.

So in the long run, it's much easier to create a blueprint to follow BEFORE you start than having to make changes and alterations along the way. That's a pretty difficult way to write, since the writing often becomes disjointed and loses focus. When you write without an outline the writing becomes episodic and doesn't have a sound structure.

Next, you construct a basic structure so your story won't collapse in the middle. How do you do that? By knowing how your story *ends*, then working backward to find its opening. The "Fade In:" that starts your script and the "Fade Out:" that *ends* your script is your framework. The span from chapter one to the final chapter is the framework for your novel.

When you're writing a short story you use a much different approach than for longer works. But in either case the first thing you must do is get focused and decide if your short story is going to be just that—a SHORT story. If so, you probably can write it without an outline as long as you know the ending or the destination.

Can you imagine trying to get from Los Angeles to Manhattan or Seattle without a map? Well, that's what you do when you write without a blueprint. It's like taking a trip without a map—it leads nowhere except to a dead end. If you don't have a direction or know how you're going to resolve your story, you will be heading for writing problems. Whether you have an outline or not, you still must know how your story ends.

Once you have decided on your ending you have a destination for all of your scenes and chapters. Your main character's destination is the goal for your story. It moves the story, gives it momentum. Many people say they don't know the ending when they start to write. Let me assure you every one of them is heading for disaster.

Would you go to the airport and get on a plane without knowing your destination? No. You could end up in Russia or South America. Would you get on a ship and just let it go wherever the current took it? I hardly think so. Most likely, you would have your destination picked out BEFORE you got on a plane or a ship.

Well, the same is true when you write your story. You have to know where you want to go and what direction to follow, and every scene or chapter you write must lead to that destination.

Let's say you have an ending, but you don't know what to do for the hundred or more pages in between. Your story is still vague. You don't have any idea what you are to do next.

First, ask yourself, "What is my story about?" Next, try to tell your story in a couple of sentences. The two or three sentences you use to tell your story will become your plot structure or your premise. Every scene or chapter you write will have to relate to these couple of sentences. They will become the structure that is the framework of your work.

When you look in the television section of your newspaper or read *TV Guide* to find out what a movie is about, you are reading the log line or the plot structure of the movie. You must be able to do the same thing, reducing your entire story to two or three sentences, as in *TV Guide*. When you read the book jacket of a novel that tells you the general story, you are reading the plot structure of the book.

In the entertainment industry, if you ever want to sell a script you will need to focus your entire idea and reduce it to a couple of sentences when you tell it to an executive. This is what is known in the business as the "pitch." Pitching should be done in an exciting manner in order to arouse the interest of those listening. When you pitch your story you need to express your idea to other people with enthusiasm, clarity, and focus so it's exciting and understandable.

When you try to interest a publishing company in your novel, you never send the complete manuscript. What you send is a query letter that tells the editor all about your novel in a paragraph or two. What you are actually sending is the plot structure of your novel. If you can't write your story idea in a concise and succinct manner, you probably don't have the right structure.

In my writing workshops, I insist that writers pitch their story to the other students. This gives them practice and helps them become focused. Each writer is amazed at how difficult it is to take their entire story and reduce it to a three-sentence pitch. Many are unable to do this exercise at all because they aren't focused.

After each student pitches their story, the rest of the group asks specific questions about it. If the student doesn't know the answers, they need to go back and rethink their pitch.

Everyone is always surprised how effective this exercise is, especially when they discover their story doesn't work because they aren't able to create a pitch. This is the quickest way to discover whether you have a proper structure. If you can't pitch it, you probably can't write it.

However, I have developed a sure-fire method to create a pitch without getting sidetracked. I call it the Three-Sentence Pitch.

SENTENCE NUMBER 1. Start with your main character's name and say what his goal is.

SENTENCE NUMBER 2. Talk about all the obstacles, conflicts, and complications that stand in the way of your main character's goal.

SENTENCE NUMBER 3. Tell how the main character's story ends and describe how your main character changes.

As you have probably guessed by now, each sentence corresponds to the three-act structure in a script. Create your opening, your middle, and ending of your script—these make up your three-sentence pitch. Of course, there's no way you can do this unless you know the structure.

Production companies, publishing houses, and networks have readers who are paid to read the hundreds of scripts and manuscripts that are submitted to them. When they finish reading they write a synopsis that focuses the essence of each story. Unfortunately, this is usually all an executive reads before he decides if he's interested in buying your manuscript or script.

One network executive told me he allows eighteen seconds for someone to pitch a story, and he bases his decision on that pitch. It can be pretty discouraging when you think of all the months you've put in writing a script. But it shows you the importance of getting your story focused into a couple of sentences.

As mentioned previously, for those of you writing novels, in your query letter you should be able to relate your story idea to an editor or a publisher in a page or so. And it is your ability to do so that will determine whether you'll get anyone interested in publishing your book.

If you can't write your story in a couple of sentences, the first thing you might try is writing it in a couple of pages as you would a short story. This is a synopsis and it helps you get your story down in black and white. It will also help you find the direction of your story so eventually you will be able to develop your plot structure.

After you have written a synopsis of your story and know how it's going to end, what is the next thing you do?

You have to decide how, where, and when you'll open your story. In well-structured writing, the beginning should always relate to the end. What do I mean by that? Let's suppose you want to write a murder mystery. Before you start you must know how it is going to end. You must decide if you'll have the murderer caught or have him escape in the end. Will he be arrested, convicted, sent to prison, flee to another country, or be killed? Until you know the ending, you can't write a single word. How can you possibly plant the necessary clues or foreshadow events to solve your story if you don't know in advance how it will end? How can your characters be properly motivated to behave in a realistic manner? How can you set up red herrings or twists for your plot if you don't know how the mystery ends?

To illustrate this point further, let's suppose you have a married woman killed in the opening. If in the end her husband has an air-tight alibi and says he is innocent, your story would be completely different than if in the ending he confessed to the crime and begged for mercy. Or if the husband was really guilty, but was never caught, then in the end he might be with a beautiful woman sipping exotic drinks in a foreign country. Although the opening is the same in all cases, the ending determines the direction the entire story will take.

As I said earlier, the biggest problem I have found with the beginning writer and even with the most experienced professional is that the writing is usually episodic and doesn't have the underlying structure that sets off the story and keeps it moving until the resolution or end.

The beginning of your story should relate to the end in a *causal* manner: there has to be a connection between the beginning and end of your story. If there is no connection there is no structure, and you are producing episodic writing, which is not connected by a structure and each scene or chapter has no relationship to the next, as in *Arabian Nights*.

In scriptwriting, all scenes must be connected, from the opening through to as many as fifty or more scenes. How can you learn to do that? By planning your ending first, then working backward to your opening. Just as Toni Morrison wrote: "Always know the ending; that's where I start."

In writing a novel you have more latitude and each chapter doesn't have to relate as script scenes must. Nevertheless, I have discovered that successful novels have a definite structure and all the chapters lead to the end or to resolution of the plot.

Once you have your ending, ask yourself, "Where do I open my story?" "What will be the best opening I can have?"

In developing your opening you must try to do several things. You need to introduce your main character and state the problem or mystery that must be solved or the dramatic question that must be answered. This enables your main character to have an immediate goal. And it starts the action of your story at once.

A screenplay or a teleplay is really nothing more than a search for reasons. You state the problem in the opening scene then search for reasons to develop it throughout the entire script until you solve it in the climax. In your opening something must happen immediately to set off your story and to capture your audience interest.

You must hook or grab your audience in the first few minutes. What I mean by "hooking your audience" is to get their attention. The television industry has many competing networks, cable stations, and independents, each vying for viewers. If you can grab a viewer's attention and hold it through commercials until your movie is over you will have written a good script.

You want to keep them interested enough so they won't change the channel from your show to another. That is why you often see an exciting scene taken from the middle of a movie and shown out of sequence before the movie begins. This is the "Teaser." It is shown to grab the viewers so they'll continue to watch. For example, if the movie is about a detective, the teaser might show a chase scene or a crime being committed. That gets the viewers interested immediately. Hopefully, they'll be hooked! It takes the best type of craft to accomplish this feat.

In motion pictures you want to hold your audience's attention from the opening credits until "The End" flashes on the screen. You want to keep them in the theater, so they won't leave, or worse yet, ask for their money back.

In novels you want to hold your readers' interest and attention through all the interruptions they have throughout their day. At least you want them to pick up your book again after they've been distracted.

I always tell my students to ask, when deciding where to open their story, "Why is this day different from any other day?" "What happens at the onset of my story that is going to set off the entire action of my structure?" "Will my audience know what the story is about in my opening?"

In *Jaws*, someone gets attacked almost immediately by a shark. In *E.T.* an alien is found by a little boy in the opening. Your audience must understand what the book they are going to read or the movie they are going to see is about. They must be interested enough to keep wanting to read or watch through to its conclusion. For some reason a lot of writers like to keep the audience in the dark. That doesn't work and is a sure-fire way to lose your audience. It's important to involve your viewers immediately and bring them into your world. They must have a sense of who the players are as well as what the rules are in this new world you're showing them.

If you've decided to write a romantic love story, you must first decide if the couple will get together in the end or break up. After you know your ending, you must relate your opening to it. Think of the wonderful romantic feature films of the 1930s, 1940s, and 1950s, the ones with Spencer Tracy and Katharine Hepburn, or Doris Day and Rock Hudson, or Clark Gable and Claudette Colbert. They followed a usual formula: Boy meets girl in the opening. Boy loses girl somewhere in the middle. Boy gets girl in the end. The beginning always relates to the end.

In the opening of "Kramer vs. Kramer," the wife leaves her husband and young son. This event sets off the story, but the story is really about the relationship between the father and his son. Will the two make it together without the wife and mother? This is the dramatic question that will be answered at the end.

Now that you've learned the importance of constructing the framework of your story, you are well on your way to developing the rest of your *Blueprint for Writing*. You have the ending that gives your story its direction and the opening that sets it off. You're now on the road to laying down a strong foundation for your writing. Now it's time for you to steer your story in the right direction, to create a character with a goal, and to develop a blueprint to follow so you'll know where you're going, how to get there, and when you've arrived.

BLUEPRINT FOR WRITING

1. Find the ending of your story and write it in a paragraph in present-tense prose.

2. After you write the ending find the proper opening of your story. Write the opening in a paragraph in present-tense prose.

3. Does your beginning relate to your ending in a causal manner?

4. What is the dramatic question of your story?

5. How is the dramatic question solved in your script?

6. Reduce your script or manuscript into a three-sentence pitch. Write it down and use as your log line or your story line.

7. Begin to create your blueprint for writing so you have a direction to follow on your writing journey.

LAYING DOWN THE FOUNDATION

"A writer's material is what he cares about."

—JOHN GARDNER

NOW YOU HAVE DETERMINED HOW YOUR STORY WILL END AND how it will begin. After you have constructed your framework, then you must lay down a foundation on which to build the entire structure of your work.

In your opening, the main character has been introduced with a specific problem to solve or a question to answer. That allows you to set up the goal your main character has to reach in the climax. In the case of the novel and the movie "Jaws," the sheriff desperately wants to find the shark that is menacing his community. His desperate goal—to destroy the shark before it kills again. In *Romancing The Stone*, the main character desperately wants to find the hidden treasure to save her sister. In a romantic comedy like *Sleepless In Seattle*, the goal of the main character is to have the love of a particular person.

In a script, your audience *must* be hooked by the first five to ten minutes (pages) of your story and must be involved with your main character and his goal. If you don't succeed in hooking your audience immediately your story will have failed.

When writing a novel, you aren't committed to such a definite structure as in a script. However, your main character must always have a goal he or she desperately wants to reach. By giving the main character a goal she must reach immediately, you will get your audience's interest and hold it until the end of your book.

You begin to lay down the foundation of your script by first developing the structure arbitrarily, so you will be able and willing to give up anything in your story that doesn't work. It's important not to commit yourself rigidly to any particular idea or character. You must build your structure carefully and slowly, letting it develop into a solid foundation.

You'd be amazed at the resistance writers have against making changes in their writing. In my workshops there are students who will argue, become defensive, and even a few who never finish what they start. You could say they have tunnel vision and can only see their story from a one-dimensional perspective. This is not a helpful trait to have when you are trying to structure your story. Writers who are successful with structure are always willing to make changes.

In other words, you must be flexible, arguably the most important trait all writers should have or if they don't, they should acquire. You must learn to give up the things in your writing that don't work and you must be willing to add the things you need to make your story work. Being flexible lets you create your work as an artist would a sculpture. The writer, like the sculptor, must be flexible. In sculpting, your medium may be clay, which is malleable. If you are sculpting a human figure you look at the entire body to see the overall structure. You might begin with the face and move to the trunk or the arm, always sculpting the parts in relationship to their overall structure. When you make a change in one area it affects the entire work. Be just as aware of the relationship of the sum to all the parts when you are structuring your writing. After you begin your story, think of it as if you were working with clay and be flexible when you make changes, making sure to look at the overall structure so it won't collapse.

THE CLIMAX

With that in mind, let's talk about the climax of your story. The climax is the highest point of drama in your structure. It is the goal of all the scenes and chapters throughout your story. Finding the ending of your story is the first thing you must do. The ending is known as the CLIMAX. After the climax your ✍ story should be finished. In the climax your plot should be resolved with nothing left to write. Your audience should leave your movie feeling emotionally satisfied and your reader should put your novel down feeling emotionally satisfied, too. If they don't have a sense of closure, your script or novel is a failure.

Equally important is the answer to the question: "Were you successful in achieving your personal vision or viewpoint and getting it across in the climax?"

What is the purpose for writing anything if you have nothing to say as a writer? There is none. What is writing all about if it's not to share your viewpoint, your passion, or your personal vision of life, death, love, birth, relationships, and yourself? It's not necessary in the beginning to state: "My personal vision of life is (blank)." But when you write about something that has meaning to you and is important, unconsciously your message will come through. That's what I mean when I tell you to write about something that matters to you, about which you care. That will give your writing a much deeper level, especially if your audience goes away intrigued with or at least provoked by your idea of the world.

I can't stress the importance of having the right climax. You'll probably have to change your climax many times before it works. Some writers have written an entire script and manuscript before they discovered the climax wasn't right and had to be rewritten. This is not uncommon, so don't get discouraged, because once you find the right climax you'll be satisfied and your story will work. The most important thing to happen in the climax is *the main character must experience a change*. She must reach a new understanding and discover something about herself or another character that she didn't know before. In psychological terms, she would experience a catharsis and gain some new insight about herself or another person. If your main character doesn't change, your writing is unsatisfying.

Another thing that happens in the climax is the revealing of your theme. Your reason for writing this particular story is made known through your main character. Perhaps you're against abortion, or capital punishment, or divorce. Your point of view about these issues will be revealed in the climax. In *Jaws*, the sheriff reaches his goal in the climax when the shark is destroyed. The theme revealed is that the selfishness of the townspeople caused the unnecessary deaths of innocent victims. In *Something About Amelia*, the wife discovers her husband really did sexually abuse their daughter and that she had the responsibility to protect her daughter against her husband's abuse. In the end, the entire family had to deal with the sexual abuse and not go into denial about it.

THE SPINE

After you've determined what will happen to your main character in the climax and how your story will open in relationship to the climax, you have the plot structure or SPINE of your story. This is the skeleton that holds your entire story together. The spine of your story is its structure, which goes in a straight line from the opening to the climax. Picture hanging clothes out to dry on a clothesline and visualize every scene you write as being attached to the spine as each item of clothing is pinned to a clothesline. Without the spine or structure you have no story, only unconnected scenes or chapters. You can see why finding the right structure is important: it is the foundation of your well-structured writing.

After you find your plot structure you need to tell your story in a couple of sentences, as I discussed in the previous chapter. These sentences will become your story line. A story line gives your script focus. As you start to write your story you will then relate each scene or chapter to this story line.

In a screenplay, if any scene does not relate to your story line, you don't need it in your script and you must remove it even if it's one of your best. Remember, your script can have only one story line. That keeps it from becoming fragmented or disjointed. You are telling your story from the point of view of the main character. Your story line must be written in a direct line from the opening to the climax.

In a novel you aren't as restricted as in a script. Chapters must relate to your overall story line, but you have more flexibility in fiction writing. You can change point of view from chapter to chapter, you can digress from one chapter to the next, but you still must follow a well-structured story line, one that you can relate in a sentence or two.

THE EMOTIONAL LINE

The emotional line of your story is the relationship between the main character and another major character. Although your main character interacts with many others, there is really only one other major character with whom he or she experiences the primary emotional relationship or line.

In *Ordinary People*, we see the main character Conrad have relationships with many other characters—his mother, father, friends, coach, psychiatrist, girlfriend, friend from the hospital, but the emotional line is between Conrad, the son, and his mother. Conrad desperately wants his mother's love and in the climax discovers that she is incapable of loving him. His emotional change is that he finally realizes he will never get her love and that he is okay. He discovers it isn't his fault his mother doesn't love him as much as she loved his dead brother. His mother is just incapable of loving him in the way he wants her to.

This change was brought about by his struggle throughout the story to get his mother's love. Even though he doesn't get her love, he is finally able to develop feelings of self-worth. In the climax, Conrad comes to a new level of understanding about his mother. For the first time he accepts her as she is. But his main change is his ability to like himself despite her. Conrad has experienced an emotional pole-to-pole change or development. To put it in simple terms he has gone from being insecure to being secure. Remember what I said earlier, the main character must experience a change! In the climax of *Ordinary People*, Conrad changed.

When you think of your main character, ask yourself what her emotional change will be from the opening through to the ending. Obviously, she will have to experience these changes throughout your story, little by little, and not all at once. When a baby learns to walk he first starts to crawl, and step by step learns how to walk, falling down a lot, and sometimes getting hurt in the process.

When your main character experiences a change or discovery in the climax, it will be believable and not forced if you have motivated the change throughout your entire story, step by step. If a character becomes courageous in the climax, he would have to be fearful in the beginning of your story. He must develop and struggle throughout the story in order to change.

It will be helpful if you can describe your character's *emotional pole-to-pole development* by using an adjective or verb as follows: "My main character goes from hate to love; from selfish to selfless; from weak to strong." This will help you determine the emotional line of your main character and determine what the emotional change will be in the climax.

Dramatic writing and fiction writing are *emotional writing*, not social, political, or philosophical writing. All films and novels should deal with the emotional relationships between characters, which is what people are interested in. They like to identify with them.

How people act, respond, react, and most important— FEEL—is what makes good drama. It is how characters behave with one another and how they react and interact in friendship or love that makes good emotional writing. It is the emotional story people pay to see or read. They want to be moved, to feel, and to care. By concentrating on the emotional line of your story you will be laying down a firm foundation and a strong structure for your writing.

BLUEPRINT FOR WRITING

1. Describe your main character's goal in a couple of sentences. Is it clear and specific?

2. What is your main character's emotional pole-to-pole development? Write it in two words.

3. In the climax, how does the main character change or discover something she didn't know before?

4. How is your plot resolved in the climax? Discuss.

5. How do you reveal your theme in the climax?

6. With whom does your main character have an emotional relationship? Describe the relationship.

7. How does your main character deal with each emotional relationship?

8. What emotions are at stake in each relationship?

9. Write about how your personal vision, opinion, or point-of-view is revealed in the climax.

THE MAIN CHARACTER

*"When I used to teach creative writing, I would
tell the students to make their characters
want something right away."*

—Kurt Vonnegut

TO CREATE A SUCCESSFUL CHARACTER TAKES HARD WORK AND A lot of thought. A character doesn't just happen. A character is born through the labor of your imagination, investigation, and examination. All this work eventually culminates in creating a believable, complex character.

You may only have one main character or protagonist in your story. This is a rule to remember! I'm certain you can recall a few movies and novels that have more than one main character. But in this book, we'll be concentrating on stories with only one.

Many new writers begin writing without knowing who the main character is. Several factors determine your main character and these questions will help you find out:

"Does my main character have a specific goal she desperately wants to achieve?"

"Is my main character active, not reactive, throughout the story?"

The most important question to ask yourself is: "Does my main character change in the climax?"

If the answer to all the questions is "yes," then you've chosen the right main character. Take your time in answering the questions, because they will help you find a goal for your character. That goal will make him active and give him the proper motivation to change in the climax.

In workshops, when I discuss the rule of having only one main character there are invariably a few students who will disagree.

"What about 'Butch Cassidy and the Sundance Kid?' they ask. 'What about Romeo and Juliet'?"

In these two cases there is still only *one* main character. Based on the above questions you were instructed to ask yourself, can you guess which is the main character?

If you answered Butch Cassidy and Romeo you made the right choices. Those two characters are the ones who have a specific goal, thus creating the driving force that moves the story. Each is the one who is the most active, and who experiences an emotional change in the climax.

A story would certainly be boring if the main character did nothing but remain passive and reactive. How do you make your main character active in your story? Give her a goal—a goal she desperately wants to reach in the climax—and you will make your main character ACTIVE. The goal determines the action.

For example, in a detective story, when the detective wants to find the person guilty of committing a crime, that's her goal; or in a story about a fisherman who wants to win the battle with a big fish he has tried to catch a hundred times, that's his goal; or when the chief of police wants to rid his town of a motorcycle gang before they wreck the town, that's his goal. Each character behaves in a certain way because of a specific goal and is revealed through actions as they try to reach their goal.

You can see how the goal is the catalyst that gives your main character the necessary action and momentum. The goal also provides the character's change or transformation in the climax.

In your opening, the main character immediately must be faced with a dramatic problem or question to solve, in order to start your story moving.

"Will the detective apprehend the criminal?"

"Will the fisherman win his battle against a giant fish?"

"Will the chief of police protect his town from the motorcycle gang?"

Each of these goals is the driving force that gives your story movement, energy, and a purpose. In the end the main character discovers that what he thought he wanted isn't what he wants now. He has grown and changed. His real goal is revealed in the climax.

The more *desperately* your main character wants to reach a specific goal the more exciting your story. Characters are revealed under stress or pressure. Put your characters in a pressure cooker and watch how they act and react.

One of the best ways of getting your character under pressure is to use a "time lock." Put a time limit on the action your character takes and you'll have more suspense in your story.

If a character must discover a bomb that will go off in thirty minutes, you are putting a time lock on the situation. This is certainly more exciting than if the character had a week or a month to defuse the bomb. Try to put your main character into a situation with a time limit on it and you'll create the necessary pressure and tension you'll need to keep your readers and viewers interested. The less time involved for your main character to reach the goal, the more compressed the pressure and tension. Think of a kettle of water on the burner on the highest heat. You can't see inside the kettle to the exact moment when the water turns to steam, but it surely will do so faster than if the kettle was on the lowest heat.

Let's take a character whose goal it is to get a job. If she is a skilled worker she probably won't have a difficult time finding one. But what if your character is an unskilled worker? Chances are she would have to struggle to find work, since she has no mar-ketable skills. This certainly would be more dramatic than a per-son who is a highly qualified worker. You can make your main character's goal even more desperate by "upping the stakes."

Suppose your unskilled worker's husband is very ill, her children are hungry, and she can't find work anywhere. She is desperate. We are involved. We care about her plight and her family. Will she find a job? Will her children go hungry? Will her husband's condition worsen? What will she do in response to these pressures? Will she try to go on welfare, or give up her children? Will she turn to crime to buy food for her children and medicine for her husband? That is the kind of desperate goal you need to make your script or novel fast-moving and exciting.

The important thing to remember about your character's goal is that it must be *specific*. It can't be abstract. You can't just say your character wants love, power, or money. These are all abstractions and are too vague and not definite. If your character wants love it must be the love of a certain person. You would say, "My main character wants the love of a man named Bob Smith."

Romeo wants Juliet's love, Antony wants Cleopatra's love. In *Ordinary People*, Conrad desperately wants his mother's love. Now we go from being abstract to focusing on the love of a specific person, Bob Smith, Juliet, Cleopatra, and the love of the mother.

Another example would be a goal where your main character wants justice. Justice in itself is too broad a goal and once again, is an abstraction. But if you wrote, "My main character was to see that Tom Green, the hit-and-run driver in an accident, is arrested for his crime," now you're being specific. The goal you choose for your main character is really the PLOT structure for the story. Does the character want to be a prize fighter, play baseball, climb a mountain, overcome a disease? This is the goal that sets off your story from FADE-IN: to FADE-OUT!

This specific goal gives your script movement, provides your protagonist with an objective to strive for throughout the story, and is the FALSE GOAL.

There are two types of goals a character can have—a "false goal" and a "real goal." In my opinion, all screenplays, teleplays, hour episodes, novels, short stories, and sitcoms should always include both the real and false goal of the main character, to insure depth and truth to the entire script.

In the opening of any script or work of fiction the main character should be faced with a dramatic problem or question that has to be solved or answered in order to start your story moving toward the climax. This goal is the false goal.

Let me explain. In *Tootsie*, a very well-structured screenplay, Dustin Hoffman's false goal, which is the plot line, is to get work as an actor. If he were Alec Baldwin that would be easy and there'd be no script. But his goal is desperate, because he has such a difficult personality nobody will hire him. So he disguises himself as a woman in order to get work, and soon he has a successful role on a daytime soap where he eventually becomes the star. He has reached his goal, but it really is his false goal. In the climax of *Tootsie*, he discovers his real goal is that he really wants the love of the Jessica Lange character. In the end he even quits his successful acting job. What he thought he wanted in the beginning (the false goal), getting a job as an actor, isn't what he wants in the climax (the real goal). He has grown and changed and discovered who he really is and what is meaningful to him in the end.

In *An Officer and A Gentlemen*, the Richard Gere character's goal is specific and desperate. He DESPERATELY wants to be an officer and to make it through officer candidate school. If he fails at this there is nothing left for him. This is the end of the line. So his goal is more desperate than a character who has other choices. This SPECIFIC goal is the driving force for the entire script. But this is really his FALSE GOAL.

In the climax, after he successfully overcomes the obstacles throughout the script and graduates, he reaches his false goal and becomes an officer. But what he DISCOVERS in the climax is his *real goal*: to have a love relationship with the Debra Winger character.

This is called the main character's discovery or transformation, since throughout the script he never wanted to be romantically involved with anyone. Yet, by the end of the picture he realizes her love is what's important to him. He has changed his goal from wanting to be an Officer to wanting to be a Gentleman.

In both examples each character has experienced an EMOTIONAL POLE-TO-POLE DEVELOPMENT, going from indifferent or selfish to caring and loving. This realization, discovery, change, or transformation is the *real goal* of each film.

Having both a real and a false goal gives depth to any script. Let's take a detective story for example. In any detective story a crime is usually committed and must be solved. That is the basis for suspense and mystery.

Here's an example. If in the opening of the script a murder has taken place, the goal of the detective, Mr. Private Eye, is to find out who committed the murder and to solve the crime. This sets off the story and is the plot structure, the driving force of the script that gives our main character his action. But it is really our main character's *false* goal.

Now, if solving a crime is all the story is about, it will have little depth. There are many mysteries just like that. Their only goal is for the detective to solve the crime. These scripts have been done thousands of times, offering nothing fresh and original, and aren't too successful.

On the other hand, if in the process of solving the crime, Mr. Private Eye, the detective, learns something important about himself and experiences an emotional change or catharsis by the end of the script, this is a much better character story and gives greater depth to the main character. It also allows the audience to experience an emotional connection with the main character and feel satisfied with the ending and with his personal growth or change.

Even in action/adventure films, when there is strong action PLUS a powerful emotional relationship between the main character and another major character, you have greater depth, you have fireworks, you have drama! Some of the successful films in this genre are: *The African Queen, Raiders of the Lost Ark*, and

Romancing the Stone. These worked because they included both levels—plot and emotional line—making us care about the characters throughout all the adventures and hoping they will overcome the danger together. By the end of these adventures we root for these two characters to get together.

One of the biggest criticisms of *Jurassic Park*, is that you didn't care about anyone except, perhaps, a few dinosaurs. There was no strong emotional line between any of the characters.

Always try to include both the false goal and the real goal in your script. If you do, you'll have a script that is powerful, emotional, fresh, and original!

CONFLICT

It is not enough to give your main character a specific goal she desperately wants to reach. A character must also have obstacles that stand in the way of her reaching her goal. If she doesn't have to struggle, there is no conflict, and without conflict there is no drama. Conflict is one of the major building blocks for exciting writing.

Since all dramatic writing must contain conflict, how do you get it? First you give your main character a goal and then you put obstacles and opposition in his path. These obstacles are necessary to create conflict. The greater the obstacles and complications, the more hurdles your main character has to overcome, and the more powerful and absorbing your conflict.

Ask yourself what would your characters fight for and what would they die for? What do they want desperately enough to motivate them into taking action and move the story to its climax? Inherent in the answer to these questions is conflict of the best kind. There are three kinds of conflict. You can use one of them when writing your story or use them all, which makes for even more suspense and excitement:

1. *Man Against Himself.* Examples of this are: *The Gambler*, a story about a compulsive gambler; *Days of Wine and Roses*, about a husband and wife who are alcoholics; and *Fatso*, about a compulsive overeater. In each of these films the main character is trying to overcome some flaw or addiction within himself. Most of the tragedies of William Shakespeare involve this type of conflict. Some of his most famous heros who suffer from a tragic character flaw are Othello, Macbeth, and King Lear.

2. *Man Against Nature.* This usually deals with action-packed adventure movies and novels such as *Jaws*, *Earthquake*, *Cliffhanger*, *Die Hard*, and *Alive*. The main character is always thwarted by some act of nature that almost prevents him from reaching his goal. These struggles usually involve life and death issues. Will the characters survive the earthquake, the fire, the monster from the deep, the airplane crash?

3. *Man Against Man.* The main character has a goal and another character stands in the way of his reaching that goal. This includes most of the mystery, spy, and war stories. But the most dramatic man against man conflict is the small personal story involving families, lovers, or an important emotional relationship. Examples: *Terms of Endearment*, *When Harry Met Sally*, and *Ordinary People*.

However, in all good writing the main character and other characters should always have internal conflicts and experience conflict with other characters. The best conflict includes all three simultaneously. In *This Boy's Life*, the young boy is in conflict with his stepfather, the environment, and whether to leave home or stay with his mother.

In *King of the Hill*, a young boy who lives in a hotel with his family during the depression is in conflict with his environment, his parents, classmates, especially the bellman at the hotel, as well as within himself and his fears. These two examples are not action-packed adventure stories, but personal stories with more conflict and punch than the greatest car crash. These two films involve young boys who both have internal conflicts and whose choices to solve them are limited. This is what makes them dramatic and original, because the stories are both so personal.

THE PROTAGONIST AND THE ANTAGONIST

In action movies, this conflict is basically good guys vs. bad guys. Audiences love this type of conflict because it gives them someone to root for and someone to fear. The hero and the villain are known as the Protagonist (the hero) and the Antagonist (the villain). If this is the type of conflict you use in your script, there are some important elements for you to know when using man against man conflict. The protagonist has a goal he desperately wants to reach. The opposing force that stands in his way is the antagonist.

You must develop a clear contrast between your protagonist and antagonist. If you have someone to love, you need someone to hate. However, the protagonist must not be so strong that he overpowers his antagonist. Conversely, your hero must not be so weak that he'll not be a match for his antagonist. Each character must be of equal importance for you to have exciting and emotional conflict. If they are mismatched there is no conflict. One will win hands down and then who cares?

The stakes between your protagonist and antagonist must be high or your conflict will be weak. Therefore, the conflict must be of equal importance between the two characters. The fight between them must be an exciting contest. In either case, hero or opponent, the stakes must be high and the consequences of each not reaching his goal must be life threatening.

When you watch any type of spectator sport, it is always better when the competition is equal. Certainly, a tennis match between Brad Gilbert and Michael Chang is more exciting then a match between one of these talented men and a lower-ranked player. The more evenly matched the game, the better the competition and the struggle.

Just like human beings, your characters need to be multifaceted. Every person has at least one skeleton in his closet. If not a skeleton, she certainly has to have a fault or two. You need to add layers to your characters as you write them. What internal conflicts do they have? What are the fears, phobias, hopes, dreams, fantasies that create their inner life?

Characters should be well balanced. Your opposition can't be all bad and your hero can't be all good. Be sure your hero has vulnerabilities. He must have a flaw or two so he'll be interesting. Perhaps he could possess a character trait he needs to overcome to reach his goal. Make him human by giving him a bad temper or having him be fearful or insecure. And your antagonist certainly needs to have a few good qualities. He can't be all bad, can he? Give each character a many-sided personality.

Remember Marlon Brando in *The Godfather*? Even though his character was responsible for the murder of many people, we see him at play with his grandson in his garden. We see his kindness toward his wife and children and his concern for them as a husband and father.

When his son, Michael, who always refused to get involved in the family business, eventually becomes the Godfather, we understand his change because his actions are motivated. When members of another family try to kill his father, Michael agrees to become the new Don.

This complex personality in Michael is strongly apparent during the scene of a child's baptism. While he is behaving as a loving father, a montage of scenes shows people being murdered. The irony is he's responsible for the murders occurring and being carried out against the backdrop of the church setting. This is character development at its best. We soon understand how and why he is such a contradiction.

The more desperately your main character wants to reach his goal the more suspenseful and exciting your story. I always tell my students to make their characters have the ESSED syndrome: distressed, obsessed, suppressed, oppressed, stressed, depressed, repressed, messed, or possessed. These are just a few adjectives that help describe the state of mind of a desperate, complex character. Your main character's desperation creates the momentum that moves your story forward at an exciting, tension-filled pace. You're not writing about the well-adjusted, happy non-DYSFUNCTIONAL family, like the Cleavers or the family from "Father Knows Best."

Every character wants something in a script, and each character is there to move the main character's story along to the climax. A character shouldn't be in the story unless he helps move the main character's story.

Writing is about emotional conflict and we deal with stories in which the characters have problems, thwarted dreams, passionate goals. We aren't interested in stories that have no resolution to the conflict. We can experience that in real life, working in dead end jobs, being in never ending relationships, and living lives of quiet desperation.

When we read a book, view a film or television movie, we want to escape, to see human beings who overcome the odds, who beat the system, and conquer the forces of evil. This is what writing is all about, this is why people pay for books and films, to be entertained and hopefully to experience by the end of the story, a resolution to the main character's conflicts.

Characters don't just happen. It takes a lot of hard labor until you give birth to well-rounded, three-dimensional characters. In the next chapter we will discuss the necessary background material you need to develop characters who are realistic, complex, and believable.

BLUEPRINT FOR WRITING

1. Who is your protagonist or main character?

2. What does the main character desperately want?

3. Who is your main character's antagonist? Describe what the antagonist wants and why.

4. What are the high stakes your main character must face if she doesn't reach her goal?

5. Are the protagonist and antagonist of equal power and strength?

6. Does your main character have the ESSED syndrome and what is it?

7. What type of conflict does your main character face? Do you have all three types?

8. State your main character's false goal. Is it specific? Is it strong enough to move the story?

9. Does your main character discover his real goal in the climax? Explain.

THE CHARACTER BIOGRAPHY

"You can never know enough about your characters."

—Somerset Maugham

To get better acquainted with your characters you need to understand what motivates their behavior. Since a character's actions must develop from the kind of person he is, you really can't begin your story until you have a thorough understanding of what makes your character tick.

You accomplish this in-depth scrutiny of your characters by playing God and creating a character biography for all of the major characters. A character biography is exactly what it says—a personal history and inventory of your character's traits and makeup and personality.

There are three categories for the character biography: the Social, the Physical, and the Emotional aspects of your character. As you develop each category you'll get to know your characters. Let's start with the physical.

THE PHYSICAL

The physical aspects of your character are basic, including height, weight, hair color, eye color, how she walks, talks, eats, smiles, her body language, mannerisms, gestures, posture. What is her over-all appearance? Is she beautiful, ugly, pretty, weak, strong, stocky, fat, thin?

Don't just arbitrarily give him physical characteristics without first delving into his character. Certainly, the character "Rocky" would never have been a frail, thin, studious type. If he were, "Rocky" would have been a different movie.

The character determines the action, but the action also comes from the character. It's amazing how a person's appearance affects the way she feels about herself and how she behaves. Think about the type of character you need physically for your story, then develop her so she's realistic and authentic in her physical make-up.

THE SOCIAL

The social aspects of your character involve everything that deals with his social world and his place in society. This includes his education: is he a drop-out or highly educated? Besides education, other social aspects are economic status, religion, race, politics, family environment, friends, work, avocation, and vocation. It includes taste in music, food, plays, sports, liquor, literature, art, and all his outside interests.

What does she do with her leisure time? How does she spend her vacations? Is she upper-class or lower-class? Is she an intellectual or illiterate?

The importance of knowing your character's place or social standing in relation to society is obvious. How he sees himself and how others view him are based in a large part on his social and economic position in society.

THE EMOTIONAL

To me, this category is the most important. Knowing the physical and social characteristics of a person enables you to know her only superficially. But discovering the emotional life of your character helps you learn about the person beneath the smile or mask. And isn't that what writing is all about, to unpeel the layers of protective covering that hides the real person inside?

The emotional life of your character will determine how he'll act and react in a stressful situation. If a person is insecure he will behave different from a confident person in the same situation. Until you can understand the emotional make-up of your character, you won't be able to develop the proper motivation for his behavior. Some of the emotional aspects of your character could include his self-esteem. Does he feel confident or is he unsure? What are her dreams, hopes, fears, loves, fantasies, aspirations, joys, pain? Is he an extrovert, introvert, cautious, foolhardy, boisterous?

Successful writing is based on emotional relationships and conflicts. Since emotional behavior is the stuff from which great stories are made it is important for you to understand completely your character's emotional world. You will then be able to motivate her behavior in a manner consistent with her personality. After you've completed a character biography for all the important characters, you will be in a position to plan your story with proper motivation for all your characters.

MOTIVATING YOUR MAIN CHARACTER

When I first began teaching scriptwriting at UCLA Writer's Program in 1980, I discovered that creating characters was and still is the biggest problem for most writers. Even in scripts that were well-structured, the weak link was always the characters. Some were clichéd, others one-dimensional, thus creating characters who were stock or stereotypical.

I discovered that one of the biggest problems with characterization was that the writer didn't know how to motivate the characters' behavior and their actions were implausible, inconsistent, or unbelievable. Whatever the case, the characters seemed unreal and contrived.

In my opinion, characters are the most important ingredient of any script, SINCE CHARACTERS ARE THE STORY! When I consult with writers on their story I always ask three questions:

1. Who is the main character?
2. What does the main character desperately want?
3. How does the character change in the climax?

Does that sound simple? It's not. If you are able to answer these three questions thoroughly you have the BLUEPRINT for your entire script, but most of all you have the character's MOTIVATION, which drives your story, the character's point of view, and the character's emotional growth or transformation.

In my writing workshop I have the class develop a character biography for the protagonist and antagonist. I usually give them a husband and wife who are living in a bad relationship. They are asked to create a story for this couple. At first, they try to develop a story, but they keep getting stuck. Finally, they realize it's impossible to create a story until they know who the main character is and how the story will end. After they have decided whether the main character will be the husband or the wife, then they have to write character biographies for each to motivate their actions.

The students soon learn the importance of a character biography, because they discover they can't develop the story until they know their characters. Some characters in scripts don't seem real because the writer forgets to address the most important question in all writing: WHY?

The answer to "why" is the character's motivation, which gives reality to his quest or goal. Without knowing why characters behave as they do, a writer isn't able to make them real. Too many writers just start writing without laying down the character's motivation and they all end up with stock or stereotypical characters who aren't real or believable.

As a psychotherapist, when I see new patients in my private practice I want to learn who they are in the present by understanding their past. And I start to develop a case history for them to better understand their psychological profile—drives, desires, fears, and what motivates them.

To simplify, I may ask "How did this individual get to be the person she is today?" I look to the past for answers.

When I work with writers, I teach them to approach their characters by developing a case history. Characters just don't happen, they are born. They come to your script with a past, a childhood, a family, and life experiences. As a writer you must know all about your characters' pasts to understand what motivates them in the present.

Let's suppose the husband and wife are having marital problems. The first thing the class must decide is which one to make the main character. Let's suppose they decide to make the woman the main character. By establishing the woman as the main character the class immediately knows the story will be told from *her* point of view. She will be the one to struggle toward a specific goal. And in the end she will be the one who changes.

The class decided the woman's emotional pole-to-pole development would be from dependent to independent. This would give the main character an emotional structure that has to be consistent throughout the work.

Now the class had the ending, the main character, and the emotional change. Next, they had to create a goal to give the main character a vehicle to struggle toward.

Since Character is Action and Action is Character they couldn't develop one without developing the other. They couldn't create the story and fit the character into it anymore than they could create a character to fit a story.

They soon discovered that the process of writing is to develop motivation for the character by asking that most important question, "WHY?" For every "why" they asked, they had to find the right answer in order to properly motivate the character's actions.

They also learned that in the same set of circumstances the story could be completely different, depending on the character traits of the main character. For example, if the wife is in her middle 40s and she has been married almost all of her adult life, her behavior would be different from a woman in her late 20s who has a career. If each woman discovers her husband is having an affair, her reactions and actions would be based on who she is. The older woman might be afraid to be alone and might forgive him, trading her pride for financial security. The younger woman might leave her husband, since she has her own career and is already independent.

The class decided to make the main character the older woman and have her discover her husband's infidelity in the opening of the story.

The next thing they did was to delve inside the character by asking questions: What will she do now? How do we motivate her to change from dependent to independent during the story? Why would she tolerate such outrageous behavior on the part of her husband? What kind of woman is she?

Besides doing an extensive character biography on her, the class also had to discover what her past life experiences were. Where did she come from? Why did she behave as she did? What was her childhood like? They had to answer all these questions. Knowing them would give the main character a back story or past to draw from.

After a lot of discussion, they decided she had to be very dependent upon her husband because she got married right after high school. She grew up in the 1950s when a woman's acculturation was as a wife and mother. Since she has been busy raising their three children, she and her husband have grown apart. He has been developing his professional career as a business executive and spending most of his time away from home.

Her purpose in life was her home and children. Now the children are grown and the last one has just left for college. In fact, she was returning from taking her child to his new university when she came home and found her husband with another woman. Of course, she is devastated because she loves her husband and desperately wants the marriage to work. He is all she has ever known, and up until this moment he's all she ever wanted.

Her husband makes some feeble excuse and promises her it will never happen again. He tells her it was just one of those foolish things that sometimes happen to executives and their young, attractive coworkers, but it doesn't mean a thing. The wife wants to believe him and finally forgives him. But underneath, deep in her unconscious, something begins to gnaw at her. The tinge of doubt. Somewhere in her secret heart of hearts she doesn't believe her husband. Although it is still not conscious, she gets a slight awareness that things haven't been right in her marriage for a long time. But consciously she tells herself things will work out.

The two maintain the appearance of a happy marriage on the outside, but inside our main character is slowly beginning to change. She begins to realize what her marriage is really like without having the children at home to act as a buffer between her and her husband.

On the surface she does everything to make the marriage pleasant. But underneath she's been burned and that pain is changing her. Slowly, she takes small steps to change her life. She begins by taking an art class at a community college. She has always been artistically inclined, decorating her home and her husband's office. She was always the parent who created the art posters for her children's classes at school.

At first, she is nervous about going back to school after all these years, but she soon discovers her artistic talent is admired and respected by her teacher, a young man in his early 30s. She is flattered. It's been a long time since she has done anything for herself. With her teacher's encouragement, eventually she gets enough confidence to matriculate and get her fine arts degree.

But her husband objects. Being a full-time student will take her away from her homemaking duties. Ah, but there is a change in our main character! She doesn't listen to her husband! For the first time in years she is feeling some self worth and says she's going to get her degree. She is scared, but feels a new sense of self respect. She begins to develop an idea of who she is apart from her role as wife and mother. Through hard work she soon discovers she is not only talented, but intelligent.

She struggles with her classes and art projects and receives an award in the college art show. She soon gets requests for her art and even sells a few of her paintings. She and her first teacher, the young man who encouraged her, have become very close. He would like an intimate relationship with her, but she realizes she doesn't want to go from one man to another—that is not the answer. In the end she discovers she wants to make it on her own, because she is no longer the dependent, desperate woman she was in the beginning. (The beginning relates to the end.) In the climactic scene she tells her husband, to his dismay, she no longer wants to be married to him and asks him for a divorce.

Our main character's emotional growth developed from dependent to independent. Her discovery or change in the climax is that she doesn't need to live through a man. She won't compromise herself anymore just to stay married. In the end we have a changed woman who has struggled for and finally attained self-respect and a sense of independence. At least in the end she is going to try to make it on her own, which she wouldn't even try in the beginning of the story.

This class exercise always proves invaluable to the students. Through it they begin to learn the process of character development and motivation. Try doing this exercise for your own story. Work with your characters and develop the necessary past and present life history for them. Build a solid foundation for your characters, so they won't fall apart and collapse halfway through your work.

BLUEPRINT FOR WRITING

1. Write an extensive character biography for your main and major characters. Include:

   A. Social

   B. Emotional

   C. Physical

2. Have you motivated each character properly?

3. Answer the question "Why?" for all of your characters.

4. Is your character behaving consistently throughout your story?

5. Create a past or case history for your main character.

6. How does your character's past influence her behavior in the present? Explain in detail.

7. How does your character's motivation move the story?

8. Does your character's behavior seem believable and consistent with his personality? Explain.

9. Write about an important event in your character's life that affects her in the present.

THE PSYCHOLOGY OF CHARACTERS

"Writing is a Form of therapy."
—GRAHAM GREENE

JUST AS YOU CAN'T JUDGE A BOOK BY ITS COVER, YOU CAN'T JUDGE a person by the way he looks or behaves. You probably know from your own experience that the way you portray yourself to others may be entirely different from the way you are feeling inside. Perhaps you feel insecure when you first meet people, but do you tell them how frightened you're feeling inside? No. You smile, try to be pleasant, and make conversation. Little do they know your palms are sweaty and you have butterflies flying around inside your stomach. You are acting one way and feeling another and trying to get those butterflies to fly in formation.

Well, you're not alone! Most everyone feels exactly as you do! All of us live inside ourselves. We all wear masks and only on those rare moments are we able to connect to another person in a meaningful way. That accounts for the feelings of isolation and alienation among people in our society. We have a complete internal life apart from other people and known only to us alone. And if we're lucky, there may be a handful of friends or family who get glimpses of who we really are.

When you begin to create your characters you must not only think about their emotional, social, and physical aspects, but also their *internal life*. Ask yourself if your character is behaving like an extrovert, but is really feeling shy inside? Do you have a beautiful female character who feels ugly inside? Is your character a mild-mannered young man, just waiting to explode?

Think of all your characters as you would of your fellow human beings. Give them the same internal problems real humans have so they will come alive. You need to develop the psychology of your characters to avoid the stereotypical or stock characters you see in B movies.

Imagine some of the conflicts you have in your everyday life—feelings of self-doubt, insecurity, lust, hate, love, pain, loneliness, depression, and rage. To be alive is to feel! Feelings are the true barometer of who you really are. What are your character's hopes? What does he fear? What is he struggling for? What does he desperately want? How does she feel inside about herself? Is she confident, insecure, doubtful, narcissistic, secure, afraid, angry, egotistical? Can you find the right adjectives to best describe your character? Look in a thesaurus and make a list of all the adjectives you can think of for your character's personality. What *one* adjective best suits his overall personality? Which adjective describes your character's most prominent personality trait? Write it down and when you put your character in situations, think of the adjective that best describes her. This will give you a handle to capture the essence of your character and find her core. Do this for all of your characters and you will see how consistent and realistic they will become.

Think of some of your favorite films, novels, and television programs. Who are some of the major characters you remember and like? Do you understand why each character is unique? Do you understand what makes one sitcom or hour episode stand out from all the rest? IT'S THE CHARACTERS!

Think of the success of sitcoms like "Cheers," "Taxi," "Rosanne," "Empty Nest," "I Love Lucy," and "Seinfeld," to name a few. Using this method, try to describe the various character traits of each actor. List them on a piece of paper and next to each name write down the best adjective or adverb you can think of. By doing that you'll discover that each major role can be described by a major characteristic, which creates the character's motivation, conflict, and dialogue. By using this method your characters will be memorable, focused, and consistent. What would you put down as a major characteristic for some of the characters in "Cheers"? Sam, Rebecca, Norm, Carla, Diane, Woody, Coach, Cliff? These characters are so well developed and layered that you probably were able to immediately think of the most accurate description for each one.

Let's face it, there are no new plots under the sun. There are only characters who make a sitcom stand out from all the rest. Look at the success of "Seinfeld." It has almost no plot, yet the popularity of the wonderfully unique and quirky characters have made it a success. Don't you just love visiting George, Elaine, Kramer, and Jerry to see what wonderful nonissues they'll be discussing each week? The characters are fabulous and they aren't the same tired, clichéd ones you see on most sitcoms.

The successful characters on sitcoms display many other personality traits beside the major one. This is why they are complex characters, rather than clichéd and stereotypical. By following the above suggestions you will create multifaceted characters with many personality traits, yet having a basic spine or core.

After you have thought about all of his internal feelings, you need to find out why your character feels as he does. To discover the answer to "why" means you must go deeply into your character's past, asking all kinds of pertinent questions along the way.

Just as a psychologist asks questions of a patient to get a case history, you must ask questions of your character to get his past history. Who raised him? Did she have a happy childhood? Where did she grow up? Were his parents divorced or were they happily married? Did he have any brothers or sisters or was he the only child? Was she the oldest child or the youngest? In school did he have a lot of friends? Was she a loner? Was he popular and did he belong to the "in" crowd or was he the class "nerd"? Did she date or didn't she like boys? Did he get good grades or was he a poor student? How did she get along with her parents, siblings, friends, relatives?

Keep asking these types of in-depth questions to get a vivid past life for your character, right up until the time you first introduce him in your story. Your character does not live in a vacuum and he must have a history that you develop. To learn his history you must play psychologist. You need to discover why he acts as he does in the present by studying his past.

By the time you finish creating a personal life for each character, you will know his parents, grandparents, and even great-grandparents. By developing a history for your character, you will be able to understand his present behavior and develop the necessary motivations for his present actions.

As a writer behaving like a psychologist you are always probing more deeply inside your character's skin, always questioning his behavior. You are searching for reasons for his actions and creating motivation for them.

Let's suppose your character is hungry. Being hungry will motivate him to find food. Hunger is the stimulus and finding food is his response. This is easy enough to understand. He might simply open the refrigerator or freezer and grab something to eat. If they are both empty he could go to a restaurant or store and buy some food. These are easy solutions to the problem of being hungry. But what if he doesn't have any food in his home? What if he doesn't have a home? What if he doesn't have any money to purchase food? What will he do?

Now you must consider not only a character's motivation (hunger), you must also consider his internal makeup. If he is amoral or asocial he might break into a house, or mug someone to get money for food. If he is moralistic and doesn't believe in breaking the law, he might ask his friends to lend him money for food. If he is resourceful, he might go fishing or hunting and use his environment to find food. If he is a manipulator he might devise a scheme to bring him a quick buck for food.

His value system, his beliefs, his past experiences, his abilities, and his personality will determine his behavior when he is faced with a specific stimulus like hunger.

Yet there is another aspect to his motivation. It is the *degree* of hunger that determines the lengths he will go to to obtain food. With that in mind, don't ever say, "My character would never steal."

93

Given the right set of circumstances, enough desperation, and a hostile environment, you can motivate your character to steal in a way that would be believable. It's amazing what human beings are capable of under the right circumstances, especially in life and death situations. Given proper motivation and the right situation, realize that *anything* is possible with your character.

The way your character satisfies his needs depends on what choices are available to him at a given time. What if he is hungry and happens to be in prison or in the armed forces? In each case he is at the mercy of other people and his behavior is restricted by his superiors and by their rules and regulations. Obviously, he is unable to make the choices he would like to make, because there would be harmful consequences.

Remember not only to deal with your character's need, but also with how he behaves in meeting his need. This depends on the desperation of the need, the environment, and the character's value and belief system. The most important determination for his behavior will be the many characteristics and traits that make up his personality. The more complex your character, the more varied his personality traits. These internal character traits will create conflicts within your character and keep him from being a stock character.

After you have developed the past history for your character and his complete character biography, you will want to study the relationship between his outer self and internal self.

What is the relationship between your character's physical appearance and his emotional state? Where does he live and how does his environment affect his self esteem?

Start looking for cause-and-effect connections between all aspects of your character's life. Look for connections between

94

your character's inner life and the outer world. Is your character playing a role or is he being authentic?

Another type of frustration your character can encounter is outside himself. The frustration could be environmental and might include: lack of money, sickness, lack of employment, or lack of friends, to name a few. These types of frustrations are the external obstacles that create conflict for your character. They are the stumbling blocks that stand in the way of his reaching his goal. He must overcome them to succeed.

How your character deals with his internal and external frustrations depends on the psychology of your character. Sometimes, reducing a frustration can be easy. If your character is always late, he can make an effort to be on time, especially if he is threatened with losing his job for tardiness. If he is unable to pay his bills because he spends too much money, he can start a budget and economize, thus reducing his frustration and over-coming the obstacle.

Yet, there are cases where the conflict persists even though he desperately wants to solve it. Suppose he is a drug addict or an alcoholic. He is threatened with losing his wife and his job unless he quits his addiction. He may desperately want to quit drugs or alcohol and may suffer terrible feelings of guilt and self-disgust when he can't quit. He is not in control, and may ask himself, "Why can't I stop this destructive habit?"

He swears over and over he'll never do it again...and yet... he can't stop.

Your character is suffering from an internal conflict he can't seem to resolve. He might continue this behavior until something from his environment motivates him to change. Perhaps his wife and children leave him or his buddy dies from an overdose. These circumstances might be enough to motivate him to give up his addiction. On the other hand, he might fall to the bottom of the barrel and end up on skid row, a beaten, defeated addict. How he will act or react will be determined by the psychological makeup you have created for his character. Your audience will understand and believe in your character as he reveals himself under pressure only if you have done a good job of making whatever he does believable and consistent with his personality.

Your audience will root for your character and sympathize with his plight even when he doesn't succeed as long as your character *struggles*. This struggle is of prime importance when dealing with obstacles he must overcome that stand in the way of his goal.

Read books on abnormal psychology. Observe people around you, at work, home, and play. Put yourself inside your character's head and get to understand what he thinks and feels. Peel away the layers of protective covering as you put your character under pressure. Strip your character of his defenses and watch what he does.

Today, television (especially cable), publishing, and motion pictures are dealing with sensitive issues such as child abuse, wife abuse, suicide, sexual abuse, addiction, divorce, and other mental health issues.

I am often called in as a consultant to work with writers, producers, and directors on specific psychological aspects of their scripts and their characters to make certain they are treated accurately and realistically.

As a writer, it is not enough for you just to deal with these issues. You must know the current theory of these effects of abuses on the victim and his family. What happens to the wife and children of an alcoholic? What are the long-term effects of sexual molestation? How does a child behave who is a victim of child abuse? What happens to the survivors of a suicide victim? Are adult children of alcoholics affected by their parents' drinking? What are the characteristics of a codependent couple? How do people cope after divorce?

All of these issues must be dealt with honestly and openly. That is why people in the industry consult with professionals in the mental health field, so when these issues are the subject of the film, the characters will behave in a realistic way.

A year ago, I worked with a woman who was writing an afterschool special on assignment. After she completed the teleplay she came to see me because the network wasn't happy with her script. I was amazed at how inaccurate the portrayal of her leading character, a teenage boy, was in his reaction to his grandfather's death.

Rather than react to his grief over his grandfather, she had the boy go out and try to solve the mystery of his grandfather's death without being emotionally affected by it. He didn't experience any of the grieving process—anger, bargaining, denial, depression, and acceptance. His behavior was so unrealistic that her entire script didn't work.

Before I worked with her on his character development, I first worked with her on her own emotions, taking her back to the time when her grandmother died and getting her to reexperience her own feelings about that death. She was able to get in touch with those painful memories and then was free to put her real emotions into her fictional male character. Suddenly, he was behaving in a realistic and credible manner, because she put the truth of HER emotions into his character and added layers to him, making the script much better and more emotionally truthful.

With today's worldly and sophisticated audiences, you must have knowledge of such psychological issues as death, divorce, rape, incest, alcoholism, abuse, and dysfunctional relationships, to name a few. These and other mental health issues are frequently written about in today's scripts, especially the real-life stories on television, which usually have to do with murder, mayhem, death, divorce, and dysfunction. You have to get in touch with your own psychological issues so you'll be able to put them into your characters in order to portray them accurately and realistically.

You must do your research if you write about serious topics that have deep psychological effects on the victim and other members of the family. You must know what happens to people when they experience disturbing or deviant behavior, and realistically show the ramifications of these experiences on your characters.

Most good writers are good psychologists. Think of Shakespeare, Ibsen, Chekhov, Tolstoy, to name a few. These writers understood the human condition. They were like psychologists probing the inner depths of their characters and dealing with their frailties, fears, and frustrations. Each one had a wonderful knowledge of human nature. They created memorable characters who have withstood the test of time.

There is much more to writing a story than creating a plot and characters. When you begin to understand the psychology of your characters, you will be on the road to building complex, interesting characters, who will be remembered long after your work is completed.

BLUEPRINT FOR WRITING ✍

1. What are the internal frustrations of your main character?

2. How do these frustrations affect the character's relationships?

3. Does your main character have any addictions or secrets? Write about them in depth.

4. Write an intensive past history of your main character.

5. Describe your main character's relationship with his family and friends.

6. What is your main character's psychological makeup? Describe in detail.

7. List some of your main character's internal conflicts.

8. How does he manifest these conflicts?

9. List the many character traits of your major characters. Find the one to best describe each character. Do your characters change in the end?

STRUCTURING
SCENES AND ACTS

*"If I didn't know the ending of a story I wouldn't begin. I always
write my last line, my last paragraphs, my last page first."*

—Katherine Ann Porter

Starting a new script is like beginning a new relationship. When you first meet the love of your life aren't you enthusiastic and excited, putting all your energy into it? After months or years of dating or being married, doesn't your enthusiasm wane because of all the effort, energy, and "hard work" it takes to keep your relationship viable and alive? It's the same with writing. Anything worth doing well takes hard work, and unfortunately, many people don't appreciate or respect the craft of screenwriting and how difficult it actually is.

Ideas are a dime a dozen, but it's the actual execution of the ideas put into 120 pages of script that takes self-discipline, hard work, and commitment. Many writers think of new ideas when they're stuck in act two or have problems with the act three climax. By breaking down your 108–120 pages into scenes and acts, your material becomes more manageable and you will become better organized.

Today, with the popularity of novels being made into films, many novelists would be able to adapt their own works if only they knew how. Although this chapter has to do with the construction of a script, I think it is also a valuable tool for fiction writers. When I refer to scenes, those writing novels can substitute chapters. Instead of acts, the fiction writer can divide his book into sections, especially if writing the epic novel that's so popular.

In addition to novels being made into films or miniseries, the state of the art also includes best-selling novels being written *after* the film has been released using material taken directly from the film itself. During the past decade it has become increasingly prevalent to turn books into films and films into books.

In either case, whether adapting a book into film or novelizing a film, the construction of a script or novel has to deal with STRUCTURE. And structure is what all good writing is about.

By now your *Blueprint for Writing* is almost complete. You've laid the foundation, structured the framework, planned your story, and created your characters. Now, you need to develop your blueprint into a definite construction.

When you build a home it must have a plan showing the number of floors and the layout. When you construct your script it *must* have a layout. The floor plan for your script must be made up of scenes and acts.

The average length of a motion picture or television movie is approximately ninety minutes to two hours. Knowing this approximate time limit is helpful, because it will guide you to write the correct number of pages for your script.

Each page of script equals about a minute of film, so a script with 120 pages would be a two-hour film. The average length of any television movie or motion picture script is from 108 to 120 pages. Don't bother writing a 300-page script, because no one will read it. They will have neither the time nor the inclination and they'll know you are a beginner who didn't study the craft of screenwriting.

THE SCENE

What is a scene? A scene is a unit of drama just as a brick is a unit of a building. You lay out each scene as you would bricks on a building. Each scene is laid down upon the scene preceding it, just as each brick is laid upon another. By constructing your scenes that way you build a solid foundation for all the scenes in your script. Every scene you write must be connected, from your opening scene that sets up the problem through the climactic scene that ends your script.

A scene, like your script, has a beginning, a middle, and an end. You can think of each scene as a mini script having all the same elements. In other words, your scene starts at one point of action and leads to another, which is the climax or end of your scene. As in a script, you need to know the ending of your scene first before you start writing it, then work backwards from your ending to the opening.

Every scene has a *purpose*. Without a purpose, the scene doesn't work. Before any students in class write a scene, I have them ask, "What is the purpose of this scene?" "Can you tell your scene in a sentence or two?"

Finding the purpose of your scene will help give it focus. Perhaps the purpose of your scene is to introduce a love interest, show a crime being committed, or plant a necessary clue for a detective to discover. Knowing your purpose keeps your writing solid and on track and gives you a direction to follow.

If you're writing a scene that shows a man taking a woman on a first date, where is the best place to start the scene? The best place to start your scene is in the middle of the action! The couple on a first date could be sitting together in a restaurant having dinner. Or they could be driving in his car on the way to a party. You would never start your scene showing him driving to her apartment, parking the car, walking down the street to the apartment entrance, ringing the bell to enter, waiting for the elevator, riding the elevator to her floor, knocking at her door, and introducing himself to her when she opens the door. This is all unnecessary and boring. Who cares how he gets to her apartment? It would slow down your story and waste time because NOTHING IS HAPPENING!

On the other hand, if you want to show something happening to the man on the way to her apartment, then you need to start the scene with him going to it. Maybe on the way to her apartment the man gets mugged or he sees a robbery in progress. Then it would be necessary to open the scene showing him on his way to pick her up, if that is the purpose of your scene. It is necessary for you to know what you want to accomplish in the scene *before* you start writing. If you can't state the purpose in a sentence or two, then rethink your scene or eliminate it because it isn't focused.

All scenes have a beginning, a middle, and an end, but they must also have a direction. When you start a scene it must go somewhere. By the end of the scene the character is at a higher point of drama than before. All scenes must have a climax or ending that leads the character to the next scene, otherwise what you're writing is episodic and without direction or structure.

Since film is visual, all scenes must have movement throughout the script. In the climax of a scene something must happen, just as it happens in the climax of a script. The climax of your scene must be the most dramatic point and further the action along to the next scene. It should thrust your story forward, compelling the audience to ask, "What's going to happen next?"

All scenes must have DRAMATIC CONFLICT! Without conflict you have nothing but conversation. Since the audience is interested in emotional relationships, conflict should be emotional conflict between characters. Conflict doesn't have to consist of battles, fights, or wars. Conflict can involve the main character wanting something, and someone or something standing in the way of his getting what he wants. That adds dramatic tension and suspense to all your scenes. A man driving a car down the street isn't conflict. But a man driving a car with someone holding a gun to his head is dramatic conflict. Without conflict there is no drama. Ask yourself: "What is the conflict in this scene?" "What does my main character want in this scene?" If you can't find the answers, don't write the scene.

Some scenes are known as a sequence of scenes. They can be described as chase scenes, where there can be many different locations, but still only one purpose. A great example of a sequence of scenes is the chase in *The French Connection*. The purpose of the scenes was for Gene Hackman to catch the head drug dealer. The locations were varied and there were many crashes and near misses along the chase, but there still was only one purpose—to catch the drug pusher.

A scene can be as short as half a page or as long as five or more. Whatever its length, the elements you should include are (a) a beginning, a middle, a climax; (b) starting in the middle of the action; (c) having conflict; (d) having a single purpose to the scene.

Between the opening scene that sets off your story and the climactic scene that ends it, you may have as many as fifty to sixty scenes. Each must connect to the other in a cause-and-effect manner. Although each must stand alone as a complete unit of drama, it must also evolve from the scene that preceded it and lead to the one that follows it. This is CAUSAL writing. One scene causes the next. All the scenes in a script or the chapters in a book build upon one another to develop the plot structure. If you remove one of the scenes or chapters, the entire structure could collapse.

Compare this to a building that would topple over if you removed one of the floors. If removing a scene doesn't affect your overall script then the scene is not necessary and *should* be eliminated. Think of your scenes as you would a house. Without the steel frame or skeleton, your house would topple; so would your script. Every scene you include must relate to your storyline. If it doesn't relate to your overall plot structure, don't use it, even if it's terrific.

You include a scene by first deciding if it relates to your storyline, so state your storyline in a couple of sentences. Next, ask yourself if the scene helps move your story and if it doesn't, remove it, because it doesn't belong in your script. Remember, all scenes must lead to the climax of your story and to its resolution.

After you have determined your storyline, how do you decide what scenes you need to write? Since there are between forty to sixty scenes or more, what do you do between the opening and the climactic scene? First, start thinking of all the possible scenes for your script. Let your imagination go really wild. Then jot down every possible scene you could conceivably use in your script. Let your mind expand and free-associate your ideas. Write everything that comes into your head for each potential scene in a couple of sentences. It doesn't matter if you discard most of them, it's getting them down without judgment that is important.

Then think of all the things that could possibly happen to your main character in order for him to reach his goal. Put down everything that comes into your mind. Think of your settings, of the characters, of the locations, atmosphere, the obstacles, and write them down as fast as you can. After you have written all of the possibilities, then you can start concerning yourself with putting the scenes in some order.

It is always a good idea to pace your scenes, to follow a strong emotional scene with a quieter one. Precede an action scene with a slower-paced one. Quiet scenes can be very powerful. They can be moments of introspection when a character discovers something about himself or another character. Remember the value of comic relief. When things get too heavy, you can use humor and sensitivity to pace your scenes throughout your script, interspersing humor with drama.

To structure your scenes in the correct order, you need to know the three-act format and what elements must go into each act. Breaking your script into acts will give you a blueprint. Then your script will be more manageable than it would be by trying to write 120 pages straight through. Breaking your script into three segments when you structure it gives you a guide to follow.

ACT I

Act I is known as the Act of Exposition. It is approximately thirty pages in length. (1–30) In the opening of Act I you must set up the problem to be solved and introduce the main and major characters of your film. This problem will take the rest of the movie to solve. The audience must immediately know what your movie is about or they will lose interest. They should understand what's going on and care about the problem confronting the main character. I always tell my students to ask themselves when they open their script or novel: "Why is this day in the life of my character different from any other day in his life?"

Something must happen to start your story moving toward a destination. What event or problem starts your main character on a journey? Is it a death, divorce, job loss, or a meeting with the person of your dreams? You need to know what your story is about and your viewers or readers want to know what world you're taking them to visit, what the rules are, and who are the players. There is nothing worse than reading a book or seeing a movie and not knowing what's happening or what it's about.

If your audience isn't hooked immediately, you have failed in your goal as a scriptwriter. A good way to check to see if you have all the necessary elements in Act I is to ask: "What does my main character desperately want?" (His goal.) "What is the problem I'm introducing for my main character to solve?" "Am I starting my script with an immediate problem?" "Do I hook and interest my audience in the first ten pages?"

We live in an age of "I want it now," with fast food deliveries, instant microwave dinners, and drive-through restaurants. Just push a button and you can buy anything you want on the Home Shopping Channel, get money from an ATM, and even interact instantly with video and computer games. So it's under-standable that more television writers try to hook the viewers in ◢ the first three minutes, feeling ten is too long a period or the viewer will switch channels.

When you can answer "yes" to these questions, you have the right elements for Act I. By the end of Act I, all the information should be given to your audience and they should know what dra-matic question needs to be solved. They should also have all the background and information they need to understand your story. By the end of Act I your main character is taking action and moving forward. There is no turning back. He has made a deci-sion to solve the problem and is moving ahead.

ACT II

Act II is known as the Act of Complications. It is the longest act, consisting of approximately sixty pages. (30–90) In Act II, you must set up all of the obstacles that stand in the path of your main character. The more stumbling blocks you put in his path to prevent him from reaching his goal, the more your main character must struggle to reach it. In Act II, the conflict and tension must escalate to a higher point than in Act I. By the end of Act II, it ◡ looks as if "all is lost" for your main character. The audience is on the edge of their seats not knowing what will happen to the hero.

Your main character is at his lowest and most desperate point. It looks as if he is has nowhere to go. In the last scene of Act II, he is at the point of no return and must take some new and dramatic action, forced to make a decision that leads him to do something different. He is really at the crossroads or turning point. This act is probably the most difficult for people to write. It seems when writers get stuck it's usually in the middle of Act II.

You need to have every scene build up in conflict and complications and lead into the next, building greater suspense and tension. This involves the best of craft and takes a lot of practice so your second act doesn't fall apart in the middle.

ACT III

Act III is the Act of Resolution. The shortest act in the script, it has approximately thirty pages or even less. (90–120) All that has gone on before is heading to the highest point of dramatic conflict—the climax. The climax is the end of your script. In Act III, the problem you set up in the opening must be resolved; your main character must experience a change; and your theme must be revealed. In Act III, your main character makes a discovery about himself. He "sees the light" so to speak, and learns something about himself he didn't know throughout your script. As he gets new insight about himself, your audience will feel satisfied.

All of the preceding scenes have been leading to this climactic one. If the action escalates in the second act, by Act III the action *explodes* in the climax. When it is over, your story is too. Nothing else can happen. If you continue your script after the climax, it will be considered anticlimactic. You'll be left with a weak ending and a dissatisfied audience.

However, after the climax you can have what is known as a tag, sometimes called a denouement. In the film, *An Officer and a Gentleman*, the denouement came when Richard Gere went into the factory where Debra Winger worked and picked her up in his arms and carried her out with all her friends and fellow workers watching. It was the scene following the climax. The denouement ties the story up in a neat package with a bright red ribbon. It is the "...and then they lived happily ever after." In a detective story, the denouement occurs after the mystery has been solved and you see the detectives having a drink together happy about solving the case.

Breaking your script into three acts will help you develop your scenes in the right structure. It allows you to deal with a smaller unit of work and gives you a *Blueprint for Writing* for each act.

BLUEPRINT FOR WRITING

1. Do you immediately grab your audience by the first three to ten pages? How?

2. In Act I, what dramatic problem or question do you set up for your main character to solve?

3. Write in a sentence or two the purpose of each scene you've written.

4. Write a scene using emotional conflict between your main character and another character.

5. Create complications and obstacles to put in the path of your main character's goal in Act II.

6. In Act III, is your climax at the end of your story or is it anticlimactic?

7. Do all your previous scenes lead to the climax?

8. Does your main character solve the problem in the climax? How?

9. How is your main character changed in the climax?

THE OUTLINE AND THE TREATMENT

"I usually make detailed outlines: how many chapters it will be and so forth."

—John Barth

AS YOU HAVE JUST LEARNED IN THE PREVIOUS CHAPTER, YOUR scenes must all relate to one another. For instance, all the scenes in Act I should include those that set up the problem and give information to your audience. In Act II, you include all those scenes that create complications and obstacles to prevent your main character from reaching his goal. In Act III, all your scenes lead to the resolution and to your climactic scene.

However, to break the script down even further, you can also think in terms of the six most important scenes in your structure. These scenes are your guidelines for all those that follow.

The first scene you should start with is the Climactic scene. Again, until you know the ending, you can't write your script. After you have determined the ending, you need an opening scene that starts off your story with a problem or a goal.

The other four key scenes are the opening scenes for Act II and III, and the last scenes of Act I and II. These six scenes are of major importance. They are the blueprint you will use as you begin to fill in all the other scenes. Knowing this blueprint will make writing your outline very easy.

THE OUTLINE

An outline is your main blueprint for your work. Whether you're writing a script or a novel you must develop an extensive and complete outline. The novelist can develop a chapter outline and write a few sentences or a paragraph highlighting the essence of each chapter. This outline starts at chapter one and continues to the end.

Scriptwriters must create what is known as a Step Outline. This is an outline that describes step-by-step in a couple of sentences what happens in each scene. It shows the order of the scenes and describes the action in each. Novelists can call this a Chapter Outline.

The Step Outline is essential to establish the direction of your script and the sequence of your scenes. It creates the basis of your *Blueprint for Writing*, which is vital when structuring your script. With your blueprint complete, it is easy to write your script. Developing your blueprint takes hard work.

If you aren't sure how to do an outline, start by writing a Synopsis, which can be as little as a couple of pages to as much as ten or fifteen. Writing a synopsis helps you get your story down as best as you can before you begin your outline. It is written as you would a short story, in prose, usually present tense, and helps give you an overview. It is commonly less structured than an outline and often accompanies a feature-length script or teleplay, when a producer, director, or publisher don't want to read your whole script or manuscript and asks you to write a synopsis. Sometimes this is very difficult, especially after you've completed your script, because they might only want a one-page synopsis to accompany your larger work.

Begin your outline with the opening scene, then write one or two sentences to describe it. Do this for every scene in sequential order until you reach the climax or the final scene.

Every scene you include must relate to the spine or storyline of your script. The scenes in your outline describe the essence of your material and create the shape or form of your structure. No scene should be included in your structure unless it serves the overall purpose. Setting up your scenes in this manner helps develop a fast-moving, workable plot structure.

There are several ways to develop your Step Outline. Some people like to use 3x5 or 5x7 cards to write the one or two sentences for each scene. Using cards gives you a lot of freedom, because you can move them around and change them from one act to the other. Some people even use different colored cards for each act so they can differentiate between acts. For example, blue cards for Act I, pink for II, and yellow for III.

Other writers take large sheets of paper and divide them into three separate sections so they can see all the scenes at once. Some writers use a large bulletin board to set up their scenes, others use the floor to lay out scenes. Whatever method you decide on is up to you. The main purpose of your Step Outline is to get your script into the best structure you can, with each scene moving in a cause-and-effect fashion toward the climax.

I require all my students to create a Step Outline before they put a single word down in script format. This outline is really the most important aspect of story development for both the screenwriter and the novelist. Until your outline works in a tight, straight line, you won't have a *Blueprint for Writing* to follow and you won't have a script or manuscript. Don't try short cuts. Developing an outline in the beginning will save you blood, sweat, and tears, plus months of hard work in finding where you are in the story.

THE TREATMENT

Most treatments consist of twenty to forty pages, typewritten and double spaced, a step-by-step, detailed narrative account of your story written in present-tense prose. It should include every scene you have written. Many writers prepare a treatment only after they have developed a Step Outline. The treatment is an expanded version of the outline and is written in exciting prose, detailing everything that happens. A good, solid treatment could be made into a movie, since it includes all the action in a film. The only thing it doesn't have is the dialogue.

Take time to create an interesting, well-written treatment that will hold the readers' interest and excite them. When you write your treatment don't explain or tell your readers what's happening. Show them what's happening by describing the external action. Use the best prose you can, with concrete verbs and action words, limiting adjectives and adverbs. SHOW, DON'T TELL!

Remember, your prose must translate into film, so write visually. Picture each scene before you begin to write it and translate these visual images into description. Sometimes writers are asked to develop a treatment before they write a script. Often, it is on the strength of your treatment that you'll sell or not sell your story, so don't let it be filled with weak verbs, adjectives, or adverbs. Keep the action going through strong verbs and concrete words. Forget camera directions in the treatment or it won't be a good read. If an executive doesn't like your treatment, he certainly won't ask you to write the script. Be certain you have a well-written, structured treatment that will intrigue, excite, and interest your reader.

BLUEPRINT FOR WRITING

1. Develop a Step Outline and state the purpose of each scene in a couple of sentences.

2. Write a Chapter Outline and describe the purpose of each chapter in a paragraph or two.

3. Does each scene and chapter relate to your story-line? If so, how can you be sure?

4. Develop your *Blueprint for Writing* by creating an extensive outline for your work.

5. Turn your Step Outline into a treatment. Does it read well? Could your treatment be translated into film?

CHAPTER 12

SCRIPT FORMAT

"Get black on white."

—GUY DE MAUPASSANT

WHEN YOU SUBMIT A SCRIPT TO AN AGENT, MOVIE COMPANY, OR network, it must be written in script format. The first sign of an amateur is delivering a script with improper format.

The script format is a blueprint developed by the writer that demonstrates to other people what's being SEEN and HEARD. It includes dialogue, descriptions of characters and locations, and directions for the characters' actions. This format is totally different from any other type of writing. There are specific rules that must be learned and followed. You should never submit any script unless it is typewritten in script format. This is one rule you must never break! It is essential that you use the correct format or you will not get your script read.

Your script should read like any well-written work. Make it flow and involve the people who read it so they won't want to put

◊ it down. One way to ensure the smooth flow of work is NOT to include camera angles and directions. You are the writer. Let the director or the cameraman decide on camera shots and angles. Including camera angles lessens the impact of your script, distracting your reader rather than attracting him to go on reading.

At the opening of your script put the words FADE IN: in caps in the upper left hand corner of your page. It means "curtain rises." At the end of your script type the words FADE OUT: in the lower right-hand corner of your page, also in caps. That means "fade to black." These are the only times you ever use either term. After writing FADE IN: skip two lines and write whether the shot will be indoors or out; the location of the shot; and whether the time is day or night. This is the SLUGLINE. It's written in all caps and introduces each new scene.

Write INT. for interior shot, EXT. for exterior shot, the location, and the time. For example:

INT. RESTAURANT – DAY or EXT. STREET – NIGHT

These are written in caps and are always used when starting a new shot. After the slugline, double space before you write the necessary description of the restaurant or the street. Only write what is essential to guide the cameraman. Don't write a lot of description, just what must be SEEN. The description or direction is written single space, upper and lower case. Besides description, you also write the ACTION the same way, in upper and lower case and in prose, with active verbs, short and to the point.

When you introduce a character for the first time, always use capital letters for the first and last name, with a brief description. "SALLY JOHNS, early 30s, blond hair, beautiful smile," should be enough. Don't get too detailed with the description unless your story needs a specific type of character.

The dialogue is written in upper and lower case directly under the character's name and centered below.

Parenthetical is written in lower case in parenthesis and placed beneath the character's name, on a line that's separate from the dialogue.

In the directions, always capitalize camera shots or sound effects.

If you are using a typewriter, the outer margins of your script are 15 and 75. Use these margins to write your description and your directions. Action scenes are long descriptions of what your characters are doing. When you're ready to have a character speak, double space and capitalize the character's name and center it in the middle of the page at 45 margin. Write the dialogue directly under the name centered between 35 and 65. Any directions written in the dialogue are centered at 40 with parentheses around the directions (angry). When you want to write more description or longer directions, double space and write it from margin to margin (15 to 75).

If you are writing on a computer, there are programs that will lay out your script into the proper script format. Scriptor and Movie Master are examples of these computer programs, which will take care of formatting your script.

Some other directions you need:

P.O.V. *(Point of View)* If you want to have a shot from the same perspective a character is seeing it from, write SUSAN'S P.O.V. The camera is behind the character and sees what the character does.

V.O. *(Voice Over)* is used when you hear a character's voice, but don't see him. This is often used when one character talks on the phone and we hear the voice of, but don't see the other character. It is also used when someone is talking over a scene that is being shot, but the character talking is not in the scene. When you see shots of a car traveling down the highway and you hear a voice narrating over the scene, that is considered a Voice Over.

O.S. *(Off Screen)* is used in the directions when we hear a sound coming from another room. It could be written in caps as: O.S. MUSIC FROM RADIO. or O.S. SLAMMING OF CAR DOOR.

B.G. *(Background)* is usually part of the description.

Transitions include CUT TO:, DISSOLVE TO:, MATCH CUT TO:. They are justified on the right margin, and are written in all caps. Use with discretion, because it is obvious when you start a new scene, since you have a slugline like: INT. OFFICE – DAY.

CUT TO: is used at the end of a scene when you want to cut quickly from one scene to the next.

DISSOLVE TO: is used at the end of a scene when you want a slow change from one place to another.

MATCH CUT TO: is used when you are showing a person or object and you suddenly have the same person or object, but cut to a different scene.

INSERT is used when you need to show a closeup of an object inserted into the scene. Insert is used a lot in mysteries to plant a clue or red herring.

THE "BUSINESS"

The description and action are also known as the "business" of your script. The business includes all the actions of the characters and your descriptions of the setting. Writing the business of your script is important. If it is too long and boring, you'll lose the reader's interest. This is not the time to try your hand at novel writing. Don't use excess words, use only what you need and make the scene sound exciting by your choice of words. You need to keep the business short and to the point. Don't use elaborate explanations or descriptions. Just write what you want to be SEEN. Save the flowery descriptions for your novel. Be direct and precise when describing action. Make it the best writing you can. Let the words sing on the page and keep the descriptions visual and concrete. Today, you can put more description in than writers used to have. That's because your script will first be READ before it's seen and you want it to be a good read to hold the interest of people who are reading it.

Always use the best prose you can for your directions. Since your business must translate into film, make it stand out with active verbs and strong, concrete action words.

The directions NEVER tell what a character is THINKING or FEELING, only what the character is DOING. Nothing else should be included. Don't depend on directions or lengthy explanations to carry your script. Use directions only when absolutely necessary. Remember, you're not writing a novel, but a blueprint for cinematographers to film, actors to act, directors to direct, film editors to edit, etc. This is a collaborative effort and you are the Creator of it all—the writer. Make your blueprint clear, concise, and a good read.

I have included an example of a scene written in script format. The scene has only *one* purpose, and a beginning, a middle, and a climax. From now on, write your scenes using script format.

EXAMPLE OF SCRIPT FORMAT

This example contains no camera angles and very few adjectives or adverbs, and is how all scenes you write for a teleplay or a feature film should be written. This format should be used for one-hour episodic dramas and afterschool children's specials.

The main difference for one-hour episodics is that they are written into four 15-minute acts, allowing for commercial breaks.

Sitcoms use a different format. Double space is used for the action or business and for the dialogue. The action is written in capital letters and the dialogue is in upper and lower case.

SCENE WITH SCRIPT FORMAT

FADE IN:

INT. HOSPITAL – DAY

JEAN WINTERS, 42, attractive brunette, is wearing a hospital gown. She walks toward a table which has a bottle of champagne on it and takes a glass. She fills the glass with champagne.

JEAN

Let's have another drink. As long as I'm breaking the rules, I want to enjoy myself.

SAM WINTERS, 45, slightly built, looks at her. He needs a shave and has a worried look.

SAM

Do you think you should have any more?

JEAN

Why not? If I get drunk you won't have to
worry about putting me to bed will you?

She holds her glass in her hand and pours some more
wine. Her hand shakes and it spills as she pours it.
She quickly gulps it down. Sam gets up and tries to
take the glass from her. She pushes him away.

JEAN (cont'd)
(yelling)
Leave me alone!

Sam walks to a chair and sits. He picks up a newspaper and begins reading.

JEAN (cont'd)
I'm sorry. It's just that I'm so nervous. Tell
me again what the doctor told you.

SAM
I already told you. How many times do I
have to say it?

JEAN
Please, just once more.

Sam doesn't look at her while he speaks.

SAM

He said there's nothing to worry about. It's
just minor surgery. You'll be fine, just fine.

JEAN

Are you certain that's all? Look at me.

Sam turns to face her.

SAM

Yes, I'm sure.

Jean goes to the bottle and pours herself another full
glass. She smiles as she takes a long gulp.

JEAN

I'll drink to that. (takes a sip)

When I'm out of here, let's go on a trip. What
about that cross country trip we never took?

Sam continues reading the newspaper. He looks
up at Jean.

SAM

Sure, sure that sounds just great.

He resumes his reading while Jean continues
looking at him.

JEAN

Or maybe we can take that cruise we always
planned. What do you think?

Sam doesn't respond.

JEAN (cont'd)

Or else we could use the money to redecorate
the house and forget the trips entirely. (beat)
But come to think of it you always wanted to
take a safari to Africa, and I know I'd be up
to it in a few weeks. Right? Sam? What do
you think?

SAM

Sounds great. I'd love that.

JEAN

Which one? The trip here in the states or
Africa?

SAM

Either. Whatever one you want.

She looks at him.

JEAN

Are you sure you're telling me everything he
said? Are you positive?

SAM

Believe me! I told you everything.

He gets up and walks to her. He puts his arms around her. Jean leans in his arms and rests her head on his shoulder.

JEAN

I'm sorry. I know everything will be just fine. You know I'm a worry wart.

SAM

As if I didn't know.

He takes his hand and messes her hair, turns and quickly walks back to the chair. He sits.

JEAN

Sam, why did I have to sign that release?

SAM

(casually)

That's just routine. Say, guess who sent you candy? The Wagners. I have the mail for you. Look at all these cards you got!

He reaches in his pocket and takes out a bundle of cards. He gets up and starts to hand them to Jean, but she covers her eyes and begins to SOB. The cards fall to the floor.

JEAN

I should have been home by now. God, I
thought all the tests were negative. Why
more surgery? Don't lie to me, Sam, please.

(beat)

Sam, I'm so scared.

Jean collapses face down on the bed and continues
SOBBING. Sam looks away and quickly wipes his
eyes. He rushes to her and pats her on the back.

SAM

You'll be fine. The doctor just has to satisfy
himself that all the surrounding tissue is
clean. That's all there is to it.

JEAN

(hopefully)

You wouldn't lie to me, Sam. You'd tell me
the truth, wouldn't you?

Sam starts to rub her shoulder and takes a handker-
chief and dries her tears as he turns her around to
face him.

SAM

Of course, I'd tell you the truth. You know I
would. I love you. Now dry your eyes and
let's have another glass of wine.

JEAN

To the future. . . together.

She looks him in the eyes as they click their glasses together.

FADE OUT:

BLUEPRINT FOR WRITING

1. Write a scene using script format.

2. Write an action scene without using any dialogue.

3. Write a scene including the following directions:
   A. P.O.V.
   B. V.O.
   C. O.S.

4. Write a scene using NO camera directions.

5. What is a slugline? Write one.

6. What does "match cut" mean? Give an example.

DIALOGUE

"The difference between the right word and the almost right word is the difference between lightning and the lightning bug."

—MARK TWAIN

FILM IS VISUAL, SO IT IS ALWAYS MUCH BETTER TO SHOW THAN to TELL. Never use dialogue in place of action. After all, the first movies were silent with no dialogue, and look how successful they were.

When *do* you use dialogue? When you can't show what you want through action. All dialogue must deliver one of three elements:

1. Give information
2. Advance the story
3. Reveal character

If your dialogue doesn't fit into one of these categories, don't use it! Never write dialogue for the sake of small talk or exchanging pleasantries like "Hi" "How are you?" "I'm fine."

These slow down your script and are boring. Remember, there is no purpose for small talk and all dialogue must have a purpose.

Another thing that will slow down your script is to use dialogue filled with directions. Avoid adjectives and adverbs like (happily), (sadly), (angrily), (fearfully), except when your dialogue intention is unclear. Otherwise, let the director or actor decide how to say the lines. Don't play director and try to tell the actor how to say a line of dialogue. It is an insult to the professional actor and a sure sign you're a novice.

The shorter your dialogue the better. Use short speeches and crisp dialogue. Pace your short speeches with longer ones. Intersperse interruptions and pauses throughout your script.

Silence can have more impact and emotional content than long explanations. In real life we communicate nonverbally a lot more often than we use verbal communication. When writing dialogue keep in mind your character's tone of voice, facial expression, and eye contact. Close your eyes and visualize the emotion you want your character to express before you write the dialogue. Instead of using words, try to communicate your character's feelings through gesture, facial expression, or body movement. Use these actions in place of dialogue.

One of the greatest stumbling blocks to all writers—is having the same-sounding voice for all the characters. But first, let me address the issue of why this failure is so common. I firmly believe the writer is "all of the characters," so the dialogue the characters speak is really what the writer wants to say through them. This is fine if writers want to reveal who they are, but the problem occurs when writers use only one voice and are afraid to reach inside themselves to all their different voices. I've encountered this dialogue problem in every writing class I've taught. Most writers can't get their characters to sound original with their own strong voices because writers can't connect to all of their *own* voices. That's why all the major characters end up sounding the same, and they usually sound like the ONE voice of the writer.

This is such a pervasive problem that I'm working now with writers individually and in groups to target this issue. Recently, I worked with a successful screenwriter with many produced credits, who was under contract to write her first feature.

When she turned in her script the reception was negative, the major complaint being that every other character in her script sounded exactly like the main character—dull and boring. She finally overcame her problem by working on the voices from inside herself and letting them come out and express themselves.

In addition to all the dialogue sounding the same, the next common problem is too little difference between each character's style of speech. The writers don't seem to care whether a character is a society matron, a waitress, a gangster, a teenager, educated, illiterate, southern, or northern. They make the dialogue sound alike for everybody.

Your dialogue should not be interchangeable among your various characters. Before you write dialogue get inside each character and listen to her talk. If she's a teenager in the 1990s she'll speak different from a teenager in the 1950s. If you're writing about a modern-day teenager, observe them at their local hangouts or school, so you can describe the slang and their special "in talk." Don't make a society matron sound like a prostitute. Decide what kind of dialogue you need to fit your specific character, then make it sound appropriate.

The third most common dialogue mistake is that almost everyone writes monologues or long-winded speeches. When you write dialogue, remember: LESS IS MORE! Make each word count by avoiding meaningless chit-chat. And realize that everyone talks with interruptions, hesitations, monosyllables, with grunts, "ers," "ohs," "ahs," sighs, and pauses.

In reality, people are usually so busy thinking about what they want to say, they rarely wait long enough to let the other person finish. When they finally do speak, what they say very often has nothing to do with what has just been said. One person may begin talking about a subject, while the other doesn't respond to what was said, and will head off on his own tangent.

Pay attention to how people converse in your daily life. Become a listener, as difficult as that may be. Stop, look, and listen! The only way to make your dialogue realistic is to listen to people talking wherever you are and note it in your writer's journal. By doing this you will raise your awareness to how people really talk and, mostly, to how people don't listen!

When writing dialogue you want each character to have a unique voice so they don't all sound the same. One approach to finding a voice for your characters is external. If you're having trouble getting into a character's head, try to discover his voice from your memory, thinking of a particular person or a composite of several people from your past who remind you of this character. Then find the best adjective you can for this character. What single word best describes his overall personality? If you've already chosen the best adjective from the assignment in a previous chapter, then use the adjective to help you fashion dialogue. If the adjective you chose was arrogant, make the dialogue throb with snooty phrases and rejoinders.

Maybe you used words like "charming, surface, smooth, friendly, glib." These words all sound similar, but each adjective represents a special characteristic that would become dominant with that character's voice and the attitude would express itself through dialogue. But don't make all your characters glib. Use that trait for a specific character.

After you've settled on the best description, dig into your own past and think of someone you know who is similar to your character or who resembles some aspect of her personality. Concentrate on how she walks, her mannerisms, behaviors, gestures, and the way she communicates. What does she sound like when she speaks? Is her voice melodious, does she speak quickly, make eye contact when speaking? Does she talk in a screechy voice or a whisper? What are the rhythms of her words? Once you answer these questions and others you'll manage to quiet your own voice and begin to give the character a "voice that will ring true."

One of the assignments I give my students is to listen to people talking, to eavesdrop on as many conversations as they can in banks, restaurants, on the bus, at work, in bars, anywhere. You can do the same by using your life situations as an opportunity to master the craft of realistic dialogue.

After completing the assignment they discovered most people don't talk in long speeches. They never get the chance. In fact, most people love to talk about themselves more than anything or anyone else.

Dialogue should create emotional conflict between your characters and develop a tension between them that leads to some new action on their part.

Dialogue must be dramatic. It is best when it creates arguments, fights, and explosions of emotion between your characters.

When you write dialogue, always feature conflict and tension, and you'll never lose your audience's interest.

EXPOSITION

Exposition is the act of imparting necessary information to the audience so they can understand the purpose of your story. It is vital to give them specific information so they'll know what your story is about. That helps your audience become involved and stay interested because they know what's happening. Exposition is often referred to as "the business"— or the action in a script.

In the first ten minutes of any film you must show what the film is about and who the main character is. Your craft as a writer is to keep your audience from walking out of the theater or turning off the television while getting this information. The information must flow and not be intrusive, but be written as part of the script.

In the past, plays often opened with two servants discussing all the terrible things that had happened to the Master or Mistress of the Manor. Obviously, this method is unacceptable and dated. Avoid clichéd ways of giving information. Be creative when you write exposition. Let your mind flow and think of as many unique and clever ways to give information as you can without boring your audience.

How do you write exposition in a way that won't lose your audience? With conflict and dramatic action, so your audience isn't aware you're giving them a lot of information. Have your characters discuss a problem while racing a car or making love. Put emotional intensity into your exposition while you relate the pertinent information. Give information during times of crisis—

when a child is arrested, a woman is revealed as a thief, or a man loses his job. Whatever you do, don't let your exposition sound like a lecture. Make it so dramatic and interesting your audience won't even be aware they are receiving information.

Examples of films or books with fabulous dialogue are *Thelma and Louise*, *When Harry Met Sally*, and *Ordinary People*. The dialogue comes from the characters and reflects their personalities. It also reveals the characters and moves the story forward. And in these movies, when information is given, it is done so uniquely that the dialogue makes it seem natural and interesting.

In the entertainment industry today, writers are more concerned with their scripts being a good "read" than they ever were in the past. This means the rules aren't so rigid and much of their exposition is more personal. In fact, in one script bought for over a million dollars, the writer refers to a love scene as being "so hot it would shock my mother."

Practice listening to people speaking wherever you go. Train your ear for accents and dialects. Become an observer of people as they talk, so you can learn how to use mannerisms and gestures with your dialogue. Make your dialogue dramatic when giving vital information. And most of all, be sure you have no unnecessary words, keep your dialogue to the point and filled with conflict. Use strong verbs in your exposition and make your sentences reverberate with power.

BLUEPRINT FOR WRITING

1. Write a scene using exposition, but make it exciting.

2. Write a scene using only dialogue. Be sure the scene has emotional conflict and tension.

3. Listen to people talking whenever you are in public places. Record the conversations in a notebook.

4. Write a scene based on an overheard conversation. Make it dramatic.

5. Record your dialogue into a tape recorder. Does it sound conversational or like a monologue?

6. Write a scene using different character types and make each speech pattern unique and distinct.

7. Write a scene using only monosyllables. Do you have conflict and tension?

SUB-TEXT

*"Talking about oneself can also be
a means to conceal oneself."*

—NIETZSCHE

ALL GOOD WRITING CONTAINS SUB-TEXT. SUB-TEXT IS THE unspoken feelings and thoughts that hide beneath the words, that which is unsaid, and it is the best type of writing you can create. Think of all the situations you have at work and home. How many times do you NOT say what you want to say to your boss, your friends, your parents, your children? I'm sure you do it more often than you'd like to admit.

Soap opera and melodramas are examples of writing without sub-text. The characters just say everything that's on their mind. They are up front with their feelings and let it "all hang out." For example, a soap opera character might say, "Oh, I'm going to kill myself now that Charles has left me for that young hussy" or "Life isn't worth living now that Sue is gone." Sub-text is the opposite of this type of writing.

Since dialogue has to be emotional rather than conversational, one of the best ways of writing dialogue is by using sub-text. Sub-text provides you with the tools to allow your audience to identify with your characters.

Suppose a man and his girl friend have been living together for five years and he's really getting bored with the relationship. Let's say he wants to get out of it, but doesn't know what to do and feels trapped. In obvious, direct text he might voice those exact sentiments: "I'm really sick and tired of this relationship and I want out." There's no room for doubt and no room to imagine anything else that might be going on with him. He's just saying what he feels, with no mystery at all.

In sub-text that same situation would be dealt with quite differently. Let's say he's just come home from the office for dinner. He slams the door. Then he ignores his girl friend while she's talking to him. Perhaps he gives her a grunt or two when she asks him a question. During dinner he hides behind his newspaper, while she continues making small talk about her day.

This keeps up until he suddenly explodes "Where did you buy this piece of shoe leather?" He pushes his plate away. "Can't you do anything right?" he yells as he jumps up from the table, knocking over his chair.

"Well, if you don't like it, make dinner yourself," she replies.

"Maybe I will," he threatens.

"Why don't you find a maid or someone else who cooks better?" she responds, deeply hurt.

"That's not a bad idea," he shouts, putting on his coat and hat and heading for the door. "Don't wait up," he says as he slams the door after him.

She throws herself on the sofa weeping.

That is sub-text! The man and woman are really not arguing about food. He wants out, he's feeling desperate. She is feeling bewildered, hurt, and threatened. Maybe he has another woman? Maybe he doesn't love her anymore? But do they talk about their relationship—her fears, his wanting out? NO! THEY TALK ABOUT COOKING!

Viewers watching this scene are able to bring their own life experiences into it and identify with the characters. Haven't we all felt the pain of being rejected? Haven't we all felt the uneasiness of trying to end a relationship and not knowing how? Of course we have! In fact, in most of our daily contacts we use sub-text, especially when emotions and feelings are involved.

If you think about your daily life, you'll realize what an important part sub-text plays in it. Do you tell your boss to "go to hell" when he asks you to work overtime? I don't think you do, not if you want to be employed. But you might go to your desk and start slamming papers around or furiously sharpen your pencils. You are using sub-text in your actions!

In personal relationships you probably use sub-text more than you use text. If you always said exactly what you felt, you'd probably end up without any friends, family, or lovers. I give my students the following analogy about sub-text: "You use *sub-text* when you're dating, and *text* when you're married."

Most of us go through life NOT saying how we really feel. We hide our feelings behind our masks and we behave in ways that are different from our feelings. Think about those emotionally charged situations that you have experienced throughout your life—births, deaths, illness, accidents, weddings, break-ups, divorces. At these highly emotional times, most of us are at a loss for words, and our feelings remain buried deep inside us.

Then there are the social situations when you want to make a good impression: asking a person out on a date, wanting to make-out with your date, meeting someone you like at a party, a bar, a dance, trying to join a social club, a fraternity, or organization. At these times do you say what's on your mind and behave exactly as you wish? Or do you act in a way you think would create a good impression? Of course you don't say what you really feel. If you said and did exactly what you wanted to, you'd probably get knocked down, beat up, or slapped in the face.

People put on a false front most of the time. They behave not as they really are, but how they want to appear. This is not deception, it's self-preservation, survival, which is how most of us act in our lives. We do this for self-protection, for self-esteem, and for our ego-strength.

Many of my students experience a lot of difficulty when writing sub-text. Instead of writing sub-text they use double entendre, saying something that has a double meaning, or they write dialogue with one character being sarcastic to another. That is not sub-text.

Every good film is loaded with sub-text. It is subtle, and deeper than sarcasm or small talk. When you use sub-text there is always much more going on in a scene than meets the eye. What is the emotional feeling beneath the words? That's what the scene really is about.

Read over the scene in the chapter on script format. That scene is filled with sub-text. The man and his wife never once mention that she is dying. They talk around it and make plans for a future trip. This is so much more dramatic and emotional than if either of the two talked about her illness in detail as they do in melodramas.

143

Sub-text is when the audience feels and knows there is much more going on in a scene than is being said. It is the *emotional undertone* beneath the words. In sub-text you doubt what the characters are really saying, because you know they are feeling something different.

I'll give you another example so you can try to write sub-text yourself. As you know, at the beginning of every romantic relationship, two people put their best foot forward. They present themselves in the best possible manner, since they wish the other person to perceive them in a positive way. They might be bored to tears with the conversation, but do they show their boredom? NO! They smile, ask questions, make jokes, and show interest in what's being said. But underneath their small talk they are feeling another way. Maybe they are wondering if they're making a good impression, or if their date will ask them out again. Maybe they're afraid their last remark sounded stupid, or hope they'll get invited up to their date's apartment later in the evening. They're saying one thing but feeling another.

In Woody Allen's brilliant movie, *Annie Hall*, there is a scene between Diane Keaton and him when they have just met. They are making small talk to each other and, as they are talking, sub-titles are flashing on the screen below them showing what they are really feeling. Now, that is sub-text!

Sub-text can also be shown through action. A character is saying one thing but doing another. In *Ordinary People*, the mother says and does all the right things to her son, Conrad, but the audience knows she's feeling different from the way she's acting. One of the best examples of sub-text in that movie is the picture-taking scene, when her husband wants to take a picture of Conrad and his mother together. She is smiling and insisting to her husband she wants to take his picture with Conrad. Finally Conrad moves away from his mother and shouts something like, "Forget the goddamn picture." Much more is going on in that scene than taking a family photograph.

In *The Great Santini*, there's a marvelous example of sub-text between the father and son when the two are playing a supposedly fun game of basketball, with the whole family watching. It starts out with them joking and laughing. Soon the son is starting to beat the father, there is suddenly a lot of competition between the two and the fun has disappeared. The family is rooting for the son to win. He finally does and the father refuses to acknowledge it. He insists they continue to play until the son can beat him by two points rather than one.

There is a lot more going on in that scene than basketball. Each family member is feeling many different emotions toward the father. There is the father's problem of always having to be the winner. This is the first time he has lost to his son and he is not able to lose to him. Then there's the mother's anger at the father for not respecting the son and allowing him to win. But most of all there's the rivalry between father and son, and the father's realization that he's getting older. The relationship between the father and son has changed. This is a truly great scene with so much going on beneath the surface.

People often act pleasant and smile when talking to another person, but what they are saying is really cutting and hurts the other person. Haven't you seen people feeling sad, yet they are smiling? Sub-text can be used with people acting differently from what they're feeling.

When you use sub-text two characters may be involved in what's going on, as in the case of a couple about to end their relationship. Or you may use sub-text having just one character involved. For example, let's say a man has just gotten fired from his job. He comes home, but doesn't say a word about getting fired, he just begins yelling at his kids to put away their toys, then he starts an argument with his wife about something petty, and he kicks the dog.

This is an example of acting one way but feeling another. He's taking out his frustration at losing his job on his family and his dog. No other person knows what's going on with him. He's the only one involved with the sub-text, because he doesn't tell anybody about getting fired. Sub-text is the under-current behind his actions and words. It is the emotions under the surface. These emotions can be anger, rage, joy, sorrow, fear, disappointment, or hate.

Most of us hide who we really are out of the need to survive, especially as children. I've coached thousands of writers who couldn't find their voice and helped them discover their authentic voice, making their writing truthful and unique. Most of these writers were never allowed to express their feelings when they were little children. They hid the real person inside and became the person their parents forced them to be. Many suppressed their anger, sadness, rage, and sexual desires. Now when these same individuals want to write, they complain about having problems expressing their character's emotions. It's because they aren't used to expressing their own emotions and feelings. They can't give voices to their fictional characters that they are afraid to express themselves.

So I work to get them to reach inside and start reconnecting with their repressed feelings. When these writers begin working on themselves, they eventually learn to honor what they feel and their writing gets 100 percent better. Their characters jump off the page and their dialogue is snappy and energetic, filled with emotional undertones and personal feelings.

Remember you are the Creator of your written world. If you can't reach your feelings or express your emotions then you can't permit your characters to express them. Go through your day and make a note in your journal every time you say one thing and feel another or don't say anything when you think you should.

Learning to write sub-text will help you recognize the feelings beneath the words. If you can use sub-text in every scene you'll have the best type of dramatic writing you can possibly have. Fight for sub-text. It takes time and effort to learn, but when you master it, the impact of your writing will be dramatic and emotionally powerful.

BLUEPRINT FOR WRITING

1. Write a scene using only text.

2. Write the SAME scene using sub-text.

3. Write sub-text using actions as well as dialogue.

4. Write a scene having one character using sub-text and the other not.

5. When do you use sub-text in your family?

6. With what person do you use sub-text at work?

7. On what occasions do you wear your Mask? Explain.

8. Write a scene where both characters are using sub-text.

WRITING FROM YOUR INNER CAST OF CHARACTERS

"All the world's a stage, and all the men and women merely players. They have their exits and their entrances, And one man in his time plays many parts . . . ."

—WILLIAM SHAKESPEARE

ALL SUCCESSFUL WRITERS KNOW THAT DYNAMIC CHARACTERS and meaningful stories come from their inner selves. It is my belief that all *quality writing must connect to the writer's "inner cast of characters and stories."* Anyone can learn STRUCTURE, but it is never craft alone that makes a script outstanding and original. For those of you who want to be more than a craftperson in your writing, you need to have ready access to your inner cast of characters. You have to be aware of your own psychology and your inner world—your hopes, fears, joys, dreams, and needs. *You can't give ANYTHING to your characters that you can't give to yourself.*

Too often, well-structured scripts end up without having any passion, spirit, truth, or soul. The *secret* to having your script or novel stand out from all the rest is to learn how to put "heart" into your characters and "soul" into your writing. Let who you are be expressed through your characters. Let what you want be the goals in your script.

To create characters who experience personal and emotional growth (the goal for all characters) you must infuse them with your own feelings. Unfortunately, most of us can't reach these powerful memories and stories inside, because we have developed defense mechanisms in the guise of protective masks that we wear ALL the time. Hiding behind our masks keeps us alienated from our inner selves. We become our disguise. Just like these lines from an excerpt of a poem by Dr. Charles M. Galloway suggest: "...Don't be fooled by the face I wear...I wear a thousand masks, that I'm afraid to take off; and none of them are me ...."

Basically, by the time we're five years old we wear our masks to keep us from showing intense pain, vulnerability, and embarrassment. We've been made fun of by our peers, reprimanded by teachers, disciplined by our parents and family, and we soon learn to put on our protective mask to conceal the person we really are. We pretend not to be vulnerable or at least not to show it. But the price we often pay is that we lose our creativity, spontaneity, the prime sources of our real spirit.

From once being spontaneous and free we eventually hide our true self, as we discover different roles to play, to keep us from getting hurt. Can you answer the question, "Who Am I?" including all the roles you play in your life: mother, father, sister, uncle, cousin, baseball player, Italian, middle-class, Oriental, musician, teacher, child, son, cook, Democrat, letter writer, Latino, writer, Republican, doctor, homemaker, producer, lover, student, and so on.

Get the idea? Now keep writing about all the roles you play in every aspect of your life. After you've completed your list try to separate yourself from your roles. How many of you can't do that? Do you know who you are without your roles?

Now answer the question "Who Am I?" but this time don't list ANY roles you play. Just answer who you are WITHOUT your roles. Who are you inside?

Can you answer this question or are you having a difficult time? Could it be you have no idea who you are without your roles or without the masks you wear?

To become a deeper writer you must learn how to separate yourself from the roles you play in life, work, and family. To be closed off emotionally is to fail as a writer and as a human being.

Now ask this same question of your character when you are creating his psychological makeup: "Who am I?"

What are the roles your character plays? Is he a lawyer, a doctor, a clerk, a father, a husband, a lover, a son, a brother, a criminal, an atheist, an athlete, a cousin, a scientist, a child? Next, answer the question of your character: "Who Am I?" without the roles.

What are his values? What is his belief system? Do you know the answers? Do you know what your values are? Do you have a strong belief system? Can you create your character from the inside out?

There are talented writers who never reach their full potential because they are *emotionally* removed from their vast reservoir of resources and they try to manipulate their characters from the outside in order to maintain a safe distance from their feelings.

A prolific young screenwriter who attended one of my workshops always came up with terrific stories and characters, but his execution was always clichéd and boring. He would have creative meetings, take suggestions, and make changes, but he never seemed to improve his work and consequently never had success selling his scripts.

Finally, after a year of revisions, I read his script, and since his protagonist was passive and dull it seemed obvious to me that he had the wrong person as the main character. I suggested he make another character, the brother, who was very active in the script, the main character. So he wrote from the brother's viewpoint. However, the new protagonist was just as dull and boring as the other had been. The writer was so frustrated and upset that I suggested he stop writing the script and work on something new, because he had been working on the same script for over a year and was really depressed.

He said, "I just can't give it up. I don't know why, but I just have to write this script."

Listening to his commitment, I realized there was more to this situation than writing the script, and concluded it probably had to do with some "unfinished business" from his past. We met each week and he always came in with his script, but eventually he put the script aside and started to talk about himself and how much trouble he had with his past. One of his biggest problems was he couldn't remember his childhood and felt removed from his emotions, operating strictly on an intellectual level. After a few sessions it became clear the story he was writing was about his real brother and himself—a painful relationship that had ended in their being estranged from each other. They hadn't spoken in years and the situation was never resolved. When I probed into his feelings about the rift, he replied, "It doesn't bother me at all." And dismissed the question.

I persisted. "If you have blocked your emotions and cut off

your feelings you won't be able to write with any emotional depth and you'll also never resolve your past hurts."

I gave him writing exercises and he eventually became aware of how much he missed his brother and began to deal with his disappointment and pain. During his journey beneath his mask he realized the main character, a policeman in the script, was in reality himself, and the other character, an alcoholic brother, was a dark subpersonality of himself that he had disowned. As he reached into his feelings, he eventually let the tears begin to flow and as he did his emotional writing began to flow.

This was such a powerful insight for him that it freed him and he no longer had to suffer over his writing. He finished his script in a couple of weeks.

As he began to integrate the different aspects of his personality, he also began to write from his different characters and put those new feelings and emotions that had been submerged into his characters' voices to create emotionally diverse characters. His agent immediately sold his script to a major studio and he continues to be a prolific, successful, and emotional writer.

Creating fictional characters who have similar problems to your own often gives you the opportunity to work through a situation as if on a trial basis or as a "dress rehearsal" for future actions you will take in your own life. It allows you to right the wrongs of your past. Through your characters your voice can speak and say all the things you're afraid to say in your own life. Writing is healing and I have often seen many writers get more therapeutic benefits through writing than through therapy!

By journeying BENEATH your persona or mask you'll be able to go BENEATH your character's masks to the real person inside. You can't explore your original voice until you allow that voice to speak from the INSIDE out. Just for now, you're going to remove your mask and write from the person you were meant to be by finding your internal voice, the one buried beneath your mask. This is really the only *authentic* way to write.

When you connect to your feelings, emotions, and dreams buried in your unconscious, magic happens in your writing. Your authentic voice enables you to move your audience, to get them to laugh, to cry, and to feel. The truly great artists are those who can reveal their innermost voices in their writing.

Let your feelings flow and become a detective and find yourself. Be a method writer and explore your deepest fears and give parts of yourself to your characters. Begin your journey of self-exploration to reacquaint yourself with all the characters you have inside. Dig out the ones who are hiding beneath layers of protective coverings, those lurking in the shadows and recesses, and reclaim these parts of yourself. Allow your fictional characters to express what these internal voices, silent for years, need to say. Channel your voice and speak what you must through the voices of your characters. Writing from your inner cast of characters allows you to create dynamic, multifaceted characters who are living and breathing human beings.

To illustrate this point, I consulted with a talented writer who began working on a suspense novel. Her major writing problem was the main character sounded weak and acted like a victim. I suggested she give her character a stronger personality, but she just couldn't do it, and no matter what writing exercises I gave her the female lead remained weak and unexciting.

Finally, I asked her if she had trouble expressing her anger in her personal life. She confessed anger was one emotion that was impossible for her.

"I can only write from the Victim's Voice, because I was never allowed to get angry as a child and I don't know how!"

As we continued to work on her anger it turned out her father physically abused her, and, of course, as a helpless child, she couldn't fight back, so she never EXPERIENCED her anger or rage, but repressed it.

I told her to write a scene about being angry. The purpose of it was to have her FIGHT BACK against her abuser and to really allow herself to experience her anger. After weeks of being unable to write the scene, one day she came in with a powerfully dramatic scene, filled with anger, retaliation, and revenge. It was an explosive scene and in it she experienced her anger and pent-up rage.

By reconnecting to her repressed rage and pain, her writing took a qualitative leap to a much higher level. From that point on her writing changed and a new voice emerged—a powerful, strong voice able to express anger. And the added benefit was that she started to express her anger in her life as well. Her novel now has an ACTIVE main character who has a powerful voice and no longer sounds like a victim.

It's important to call upon different aspects of your own personality which you've ignored or have not expressed to create different aspects of your characters' personalities. HOW CAN YOU GIVE TO YOUR CHARACTERS THOSE PARTS OF YOURSELF YOU CAN'T GIVE TO YOURSELF?

Remember, YOU are ALL the characters. And an interesting character, like an interesting person, is always filled with contradictions. Just as humans are capable of loving and hating the same person, or committing good and evil, so are characters in a drama capable of the same behavior. These opposing drives create conflict and frustration within humans and within characters, too.

These conflicts are the basis of the internal obstacles put in your character's path to keep him from reaching his goal. Just as you have to deal with your own personal conflicts so does your fictional character have to deal with his personal conflicts to reach his goal.

Here are seven steps to help you learn how to tap into your inner cast of characters and stories.

7 STEPS FOR WRITING FROM YOUR INNER SELF

- LISTEN TO YOUR INTUITION. Trust your "gut" feelings and instinct about your characters and stories.

- BE PASSIONATE ABOUT YOUR CHARACTERS. Know your characters inside out. Live with them, fight for them, nurture them.

- HAVE A VISION. Believe in your ideas! Feel strong about your values, beliefs, and point of view.

- JOURNEY BENEATH YOUR MASK. Tap into your inner world. Trust your real "Self."

- DISCOVER NEW VOICES. Write from your inner cast of characters. Allow new voices from inside to be heard.

- WRITE FROM YOUR HEART. Take your childhood stories and emotions and transform them into original, salable scripts or manuscripts.

- GIVE THE GIFT OF YOURSELF. You are unique and original. Reveal yourself and let the world know who you are!

You can write about many things you haven't experienced and still be truthful to a character. For example, I had a sitcom writer come to see me because she was given an assignment to write for one of the new television shows about a married couple. She said, "Rachel, how can I do this assignment, I've never been married?"

I asked, "Are you writing a documentary about marriage, or are you writing about a man and a woman and their feelings toward each other?"

She said she was writing about their relationship. I then asked, "Have you ever been in love and dealt with relationship problems? Have you ever felt jealousy, lack of trust, passion, insecurity, love, lust, and hate?"

Of course, her answer was "yes," and she realized as we spoke that although she hadn't been married, she certainly had experienced the same emotions and feelings others have, whether married or not. The same is true when you're forced to write about a set of characters created by someone else, as in a sitcom or hour episodic drama.

To make your stories fresh and unique is to bring your own personal feelings and pieces of yourself into the characters. Do you have to be a murderer to write about one, or a prostitute to portray one? Of course you don't. What you do have to do is take your murderous feelings or your sexual ones and put them into your characters. When I say write what you know, I don't want you always to take me literally. What I do want you to do is get in touch with the various feelings you know and write about them, so your writing and characters will be compelling, complex, and credible!

Most script and fiction writers who are successful can usually access their various selves and put those parts into their stories and characters, regardless whether or NOT they have actually experienced the same situation. From sitcoms to hour episodes, from short stories to novels, they achieve emotional honesty and passion when they write.

So even if you're not a mother, father, murderer, preacher, cheerleader, beauty queen, or lawyer, you can still write about these characters by going beneath your own mask and connecting with all the various human beings residing there.

Become aware of your emotions and ask yourself, "What would I feel in the same situation?" By answering this question before you write you'll be using yourself as the most potent creative resource of all.

One successful screenwriter came to see me because she was bored with her writing and felt it was shallow. She had several movies produced, mostly in the genre of action adventures. During one of my workshops, she wrote about her childhood and realized being an army brat would make an interesting script. She stopped writing for a specific commercial market and started writing from her heart, from her inner self. To her surprise, her screenplay, which she really wrote just to tell her personal story, was bought for six figures and turned out to be one of her most successful scripts. It was certainly better than any of her previous "action" films.

Dr. C.G. Jung, the Swiss psychiatrist, referred to ARCHE-TYPAL CHARACTERS as universal because they have been portrayed in every culture through the ages. These archetypes have been imprinted in everyone's Collective Unconscious, going back to primitive man, where all emotions and feelings were collected. The following is a list of these Universal characters living inside you. Open yourself to all of them—the good and the bad. Some of the most popular have frequently appeared in films, books, and television and have reimpressed themselves on our culture.

YOUR INNER CAST OF CHARACTERS

- CRITICAL PARENT—unsupportive, unloving, judgmental.

- RESTRICTIVE PARENT—distant, cold, detached.
- LITTLE PROFESSOR—child who can make parents proud by being mature and getting good grades, bright.
- THE PERFECT CHILD—does everything right. Good little girl, good little boy, obedient, dutiful.
- THE FEMME FATALE—sexpot, nymphomaniac, siren, flirt.
- THE LADIES MAN—hunk, macho, stud, Don Juan, sexy.
- AMAZON WO /MAN—capable, independent, aggressive, self-sufficient, invincible, Tarzan.
- WITCH /BITCH—aggressive, cold, bitchy (Joan Collins, Bette Davis, Joan Crawford types.)
- WALLFLOWER—*Marty* is a good example of this. Shy, quiet, low self-esteem, insecure.
- DICTATOR—the boss, orders you around, you never do enough, never gives you a moment's peace.
- REBEL–nonconformist, stubborn, rulebreaker, goes against the grain. James Dean or Marlon Brando type.
- BIG SHOT—J. R. Ewing in "Dallas," Gecko in *Wall Street*; picks up check, gets best seats anywhere.
- MADONNA—mother figure, caretaker, homebody (Mrs. Cleaver, Miss Ellie, Harriet Nelson).
- VICTIM—Cinderella, Sleeping Beauty, waits to be taken care of, wants to be rescued, righteous, self-pitying, "poor me, ain't it awful?"
- LITTLE PRINCE /SS—spoiled, wants to be waited on, doted upon, given his/her just due.
- CARETAKERS—charitable, Mrs. Fixit, helps others all the time, always at funerals, visits hospitals.
- PEOPLE PLEASER—pleases people all the time, has no needs of own, wants people to like them.

- JOKER, PRANKSTER, CLOWN—entertainer, plays practical jokes on people, cut-up, gets in trouble, mischievous, attention seeker, false face, wears a mask, hiding sadness, laughing on outside.

- VILLAIN—angry, manipulator, revenger, avenger, villain in thrillers, are safety valves to help you release the steam inside you—releasing the parts of you you can't express openly. Sexual tension, rage, makes colorful character.

- HERO/HEROINE—overcomes struggles, the dragon-slayer, always overcomes obstacles—does heroic deeds (Rambo, Robin Hood).

- PERFECTIONIST—mother in *Ordinary People*, compulsive-obsessive, up-tight.

- WARRIOR—Gary Cooper and John Wayne types, saves the day, fights off the enemies.

- RESCUER—tries to make an alcoholic, derelict, criminal find the right path. Likes to play Florence Nightingale, takes in stray dogs, cats, and people.

- MARTYR—what I could have, should have done, self-pitying and self-sacrificing and let's you know it.

- CRITIC—beats you up, needles you, always judges you, puts you down, your negative programming—critical voices from your past, your own worst enemy.

- VULNERABLE LITTLE CHILD—victim, helpless, crying all the time, dependent.

- SUPER RESPONSIBLE CHILD/PARENT—both sides of the same coin. Making everyone else depend on them.

- LOGICAL ADULT—analytical, unemotional, intellectual, rational, distant, unreachable.

- SHADOW SELF—the part of you it's hard to accept—your lust, greed, the dark side, jealous, revengeful self you don't want to admit. Capable of killing, torture, murderous feelings.
- THE WISE HIGHER SELF—creative, imaginative, all-knowing, spiritual, lofty, intuitive, instinctual.

Remember, powerful writing needs to come from inside you. By learning how to write from your cast of characters you'll unlock the door to create unique and original characters, who touch the hearts of your audience. Model your fictional characters after these archetypes. Call upon your inner cast of characters for they make up the most unique, original and exciting character of all—YOU!

BLUEPRINT FOR WRITING

1. Write down all the characters living inside you. Read over your list and keep adding to your inner cast of characters.

2. Are you able to write with a strong voice? If no, why not?

3. Do you write from a victim's voice? Do all your characters sound like victims? If yes, write from a survivor's voice.

4. Write a scene from the opposite sex's point of view.

5. Do you acknowledge your shadow self, where you feel jealousy, envy, and rage? Write a scene from this inner character.

6. Are you frightened by your angry impulses and do you deny them? Write a scene and express your anger through a character who is angry.

7. How many masks do you wear? List them. Write a scene about the first time you put on your mask as a defense to protect you.

OVERCOMING WRITER'S BLOCK

*"You get a writer's block by being aware that
you're putting it out there."*

—FRANK HERBERT

I N A RECENT WRITING WORKSHOP, A YOUNG MAN ASKED ME, "DO you have to be psychotic to be a writer?"

At first, I thought he was kidding and waited for his laughter, but after a few moments of silence, I realized he was quite serious. I began to wonder how many other people believed the stereotype of the emotionally disturbed writer, holed up in his cold-water flat with a half-empty bottle of vodka by his side, typing away in the wee hours of the morning.

Contrary to this romantic notion, a writer must have at least a semi-healthy ego and confidence in his work and himself. How else can he maintain any sort of belief in himself when faced with constant rejection? How can he continuously motivate himself to write, when nothing he has written has been sold? How can he keep on going when there's no positive reinforcement to spur him on? This is a pretty formidable task even for a very secure person to accomplish, let alone someone with a fragile ego.

Through the years I have counseled writers when they became blocked, so I have seen different types of writer's blocks. This one-to-one counseling has given me tremendous insight into the myriad causes of writer's block, some of which are obvious, others less so. Some writers successfully overcome their blocks, others remain immobilized, unable to write at all.

Many writers are blocked every day when they first start to write, especially if they're writing a new scene or chapter. One good way to get yourself unblocked when you start to write is NOT to start writing a new scene, but to stop your work in the middle just before you end the scene you're working on. Then, the next time you start writing all you'll have to do is finish writing the scene you've been working on. This gets you started immediately before you begin to worry about a new scene.

The next time you write, instead of being blocked by having to switch gears with new material, you'll start writing immediately because you'll know exactly where you're going and how to get there.

You also can keep yourself from being blocked from starting your work by actually retyping or rewriting a couple of pages you already have written. That gets you back into the rhythm of your words and your writing will just flow right into the next scene.

To some writers who get blocked by facing an empty page I suggest they lightly put marks on the page with a pencil, then they won't face a "blank" page. It's also a good idea to read your favorite poetry for ten to fifteen minutes before you start to write. This gets your mind into the meter and rhythm of the poems and relaxes you, quieting your questioning mind.

These are rather basic techniques for overcoming writer's block, but sometimes it can be a very complex phenomenon, and not easy to break through.

When I consult with writers who are blocked I always try to find out first what's going on in their life while they're working on their script. That helps me determine whether the problem is with the WRITING or the WRITER.

Often writers who have been working on a project, literally for years, are so stuck and blocked they feel trapped and immobilized. Many times, after talking to them, I find the problem has nothing at all to do with their writing, but everything to do with what's going on in their lives at the moment.

Since I strongly believe you can't separate the writer from the writing (except when you have to sell your work), it's imperative to find the root cause of the problem before I recommend how to overcome the block.

Recently, an award-winning writer came to see me upon finishing her script, because she was blocked and couldn't do the rewrite. She said, "I can't believe it! I wrote my screenplay without a main character! Every other character is interesting and exciting and my main character is inactive and boring. She's a victim. She isn't there. She's just an empty shell."

During our session, as we discussed the script and why she was blocked, it became clear the story was very autobiographical. When I pointed out similarities between the main character and herself, she resisted my insight because she didn't want to connect with an aspect of her personality she had tried hard to disown.

So she kept feeling blocked and couldn't get a handle on the main character because she was too close to be objective. Her blind spot was exactly the same one her heroine had and her character's life mirrored her own and had the exact same issues. As we worked together on her current life problem she was resistant and remained blocked. But as we continued, she started working on resolving her current problems. One day she blurted, "My God, the main character's me!"

Finally, this writer was willing to look at herself and risk dealing with aspects of her life that were uncomfortable and hurtful. By having the courage to realize the connection between herself and her main character, she overcame her block as she solved her own personal problem. Of course, then she solved the problem in her script and quickly rewrote it!

There are many variables with writer's block. A writer's frame of mind is so important to his work that a simple solution to "Why do I have writer's block?" is never possible.

Recently, a writer who wanted advice on craft consulted me because he was blocked and couldn't finish the last part of his novel. He was panicked because he had a deadline from his publisher. After I read his novel I asked him, "Is there anything in the writing that's bringing up some unfinished business from your past?"

He talked about how he felt when he worked on his manuscript and told me about a particular childhood issue that kept surfacing during the writing. Together we discussed this "unfinished business," and he was finally able to overcome his block and quickly finish his novel.

His block came from his own RESISTANCE to the material he was working on and from the repressed feelings that came up during the writing. To his credit, he didn't give up, but kept working hard until he broke through the block. The interesting point is this writer took childhood material that originally caused him pain and transformed it into an arena of conflict between his characters. By writing from his childhood stories he was able to let go of the painful memories and work through his block. This fictional conflict turned out to be one of the high points of drama in his novel. He wrote from his heart and created a dynamic novel.

Sometimes writer's block is caused by the cruelty or insensitivity of other people. Several years ago, a young woman came up to me after a writing workshop and thanked me for helping her with her writing.

"I'm so grateful to you for making the workshop a 'safe place' to read my work."

I asked her why.

She confessed. "I haven't written for over five years and this is the first time I was able to write anything. I had a writing teacher who tore my script apart in front of the entire class. I was humiliated by his remarks. Maybe he didn't realize how he hurt me, but ever since then I lost all my confidence and haven't been able to write."

Few writers escape being blocked at some time during their writing career by taking workshops or participating in writing groups. It's important for you not to let any teacher, colleague, friend, or family member be destructive in their criticism of your work. Constructive criticism is fine, especially when someone makes a suggestion targeted to a specific writing problem. That is the only type of criticism I ever permit in my classes. Don't ever allow anyone to say, "Your writing stinks" "That isn't any good" "You can't write."

If you take a class and that happens with the teacher or another student, RUN, don't walk to the nearest exit and ask for your money back. Often writer's block has nothing to do with thoughtless or insensitive criticism, but can develop from the fragile balance the writer needs to maintain motivation and enthusiasm in the face of self-doubt and self-criticism.

From my perspective as a psychotherapist AND writing teacher, I make diagnoses based on whether or not the block is one of craft or personality. There are many reasons people become blocked and no blocks can be treated the same. Working with blocks is as unique as individual writers.

There are personal blocks that affect your work—blocks emanating from problems such as drinking, addictions, divorce, financial pressures, family dysfunctions, and relationship problems.

Then there are working environments that create blocks: deadlines, worry about results, stress, poor working conditions, job insecurity, ratings, negative environment, the bottom line, and fear of being only as good as your last sale or being rejected.

In other cases, writers may use writer's block to focus all their energy on the writing to avoid dealing with other problems in their lives. Maybe they have a bad personal relationship, are suffering from depression, or feel stuck in a "going-nowhere" job. By developing writer's block and obsessing over it, they can ignore what's really bothering them. The block can be a form of avoidance, protecting them from failure, pain, and rejection.

Sometimes the reasons you have for being blocked and not writing have nothing to do with writing. They are merely excuses to rationalize what you are too afraid to face. These blocks often stem from an unconscious need for self-protection. How can you be rejected if you don't write? How can you get hurt if you're not criticized? How can you be a failure if you can't produce?

Fear may be all encompassing when you are a writer. There are often psychological causes for blocks that emerge from internal forces such as insecurity, fear of failure, fear of success, fear of rejection, negative self-talk, unrealistic expectations, procrastination, depression, and repressed emotions. These are all defenses against fear.

But suppose you aren't developing writer's block as a defense mechanism. Suppose you desperately want to write—more than anything in the world. You sit at your typewriter or computer day after day and you can't. You feel frustrated, depressed and your life is unbearable, because you can't do the thing you love to do most—WRITE. You stare at the blank page and panic. Where to start? What to write? A small voice whispers in your ear, "You don't have anything exciting to say. "

The voice gets louder as it laughs, "Look who's trying to write. You know it'll be rejected! "

Soon the laughter drowns out your thoughts and ideas and you aren't able to produce any words onto the empty page. Every day you go to your computer or your typewriter to write and the well is dry. *If this is the case you are truly blocked!*

I have identified the following six stumbling blocks that keep writers from succeeding with their writing, all of which are different aspects of FEAR!

6 STUMBLING BLOCKS TO WRITING

1. procrastination
2. fear of success/failure
3. fear of rejection
4. psychological and creative blocks
5. inner critic
6. negative frame of mind

These culprits are responsible for most of the problems writers experience when they sit down to write and become immobilized. These blocks are responsible for preventing writers from getting started and from finishing their projects, for keeping them stuck in the middle of their work, for creating resistance to writing itself, for diminishing belief in one's talent and ability, for preventing writers from getting their work into the marketplace, for causing low self-esteem and insecurity, decreasing creativity, increasing stress, and depression.

Next to each block write about how each affects you? From which of these do you suffer the most? All of them? None? Some? Identifying your block is the first step to overcoming it.

Next, rate each block from 1–6, the worst being number 1. After you've written how the symptoms block you, you are on the path toward overcoming them because you are now AWARE of what specific blocks you have. This awareness is the first step to overcoming a problem. The second step is writing anyway. Just write despite the block.

Although all these states can cause writer's block, the two most prevalent are "procrastination" and "the inner critic." They are the two biggest stumbling blocks to writing success. The most common reasons for procrastination are usually psychological and unconscious—hidden from the writer's awareness. You desperately want to write and yet don't, causing you great pain and suffering.

On a conscious level, sometimes people aren't willing to put in the hard work and the discipline to overcome blocks. This internal conflict may stem from your fear of failure or even fear of success. These fears will unconsciously sabotage any long-term attempt to keep working on a script or novel and manifest themselves in the form of procrastination. They not only prevent you from completing your writing, but eventually lead you to feelings of low self-esteem, guilt, and shame.

Your internal message or script may say to you, "Why don't you have any discipline or will-power?" "Why can't you set goals and reach them?" and the questions remain unanswered, because the real reasons are safely hidden away in your unconscious, just waiting to attack you when you least expect it.

These fears are probably related to your childhood when a parent or teacher said, "That's not the way to do it." or "Can't you ever get anything right?" "Why can't you be perfect?" After all if you don't write you won't be rejected.

Although these scripts or messages are different from fear of success, they all stem from the same source. Your inner dialogue says, "You don't deserve to be successful." or "You aren't good enough to make it." In either case the outcome is the same—you procrastinate.

Another reason writers procrastinate is they have what is called low frustration tolerance. These people can never deal with frustrating situations or tasks, so they look for ways to avoid taking action, which means they avoid writing. Instead, they divert themselves with activities that provide immediate gratification and escape: eating, drinking, going to movies, talking on the phone, or watching television. These activities take no discipline or concentration and relieve the writer's inner anxiety so the writer doesn't have to put in the long hours required to master the craft of writing.

One of the best ways to overcome procrastination is to enter therapy and explore your memories, dreams, and unconscious and bring these negative messages into your awareness. However, a more direct way to overcome procrastination is your own behavior—ACT! When you act against your fears you start to conquer them. Don't think about writing, fantasize about it, worry about it, or feel guilty about it—DO IT! Suddenly, you'll find that all the time and energy you wasted procrastinating, you'll be using to get your writing done.

Imagine if you will that you are about to sit down and write when suddenly you're stopped in your tracks by the voice of your INNER CRITIC. Whenever that happens you know you feel frustrated, lonely, angry, depressed, hopeless, and helpless, asking yourself if you'll ever write again. You feel out of control and don't know where to turn. Let's look at some steps you can take to shut up your inner critic.

The first thing you want to do is identify the inner voice who talks to you all the time—the voice that's filled with criticism, self-doubt, and negativity. This may be the voice of a critical parent, your peers, or your teachers. It's a voice you have integrated into your own critical voice. It stops you before you even get started writing. It fills you with insecurity and doubt about your ability to write. It damages your self-esteem and blocks your creativity.

What can you do about it? How can you get rid of it? One of the successful techniques I have developed is to have writers list on paper all the negative self-talk they hear whenever they start to write. Why don't you do that. Right now! When you hear the voice, immediately write down whatever it's saying to you. It could say things like:"Get a real job." "Look who's trying to be a writer." "You have nothing new to say." "There are too many good books already written." "Get serious! You can't write."

These are a few examples of the put downs you say to yourself before you even start to write. All these negative sayings and self-talk makes it almost impossible to write. They stop you in your tracks before you even get started, so you have to know how you're stopping yourself by jotting down your negative self-talk as fast as you can as you're experiencing it. Read over everything you've written. Is all of it true? Part of it? None of it?

Write down all the negative self-talk your inner critic says to you. Fill the entire page and recognize whose voice is talking to you. The first step you take to break through your block is to identify the voice! Whose voice is it—mother's, father's, relatives, peers, teacher's? Or is the voice a combination of all of them?

After you've identified the person or persons saying all those negative things about you, write down their name next to each negative remark. Read over the criticisms once again. Now ask yourself if what they're saying about you is true?

Next, take a clean sheet of paper and write a dialogue with the person(s) who said all those horrible things about you and your ability. Tell them all the things you wanted to say, but never had the courage. Let them know how you feel about what they've said to you and how it has hurt you all these years. After you've written to them you'll probably realize how silly and ridiculous it is for you to allow people from your past to keep their power over you. Don't let their criticisms stop you in your tracks when you want to write. Realize that the voice is not telling you the truth, so you can take away its power to block you.

Carry a notebook and record your negative self-talk every time you hear it. (I imagine you'll be writing most of the day at first.) By writing down the criticisms you will see how insidious your negative self-talk is and what a hold it has on your writing and on your self-esteem. To counteract the negative remarks, continue to write positive statements next to them. You've been carrying around this critical voice all these years and now is the time to let go of your inner critic and to silence it by refuting what it says.

Take away its power and give your creativity back to yourself. Create a written list of positive statements about yourself as a writer and read them over until you memorize them. Use them to silence your inner critic the moment it begins to criticize you. Remember, that inner critic has had a full-time job criticizing your writing and you, so you must be vigilant in your counterattack. Next time the "inner critic" starts shouting negatives to you— IGNORE IT! Tell it to "shut up!"

For twenty-one days read your positive list over every morning when you wake up and every evening before going to bed until you believe what it says. If *you* don't believe in yourself and take yourself seriously as a writer, who will? These techniques really work and writers have overcome blocks by working hard and diligently to break through them.

Breaking free from blocks can be an exciting, exhilarating experience! When you overcome your writer's or writing block a wonderful thing happens—you'll feel a new sense of "lightness" and freedom when you write. Here are ten keys you can use to open your blocks. Writer's block is really pent-up creative energy. When you break free from your blocks a tremendous amount of this stored-up creativity will come bursting forth. Overcoming blocks gives you freedom to make your writing a joyful experience, where you are having fun with words, excitement with your ideas, and pleasure in the writing process!

BLUEPRINT FOR WRITING

1. Stay in the moment

2. Suspend critical judgments

3. Be open to all possibilities

4. Forget about results

5. Silence your "Inner Critic"

6. Be in the process and not the product

7. Embrace your playful child

8. Lose your "self"

9. Be courageous

10. Reveal yourself

THE FINISHED PRODUCT

*"I usually have a sense of clinical fatigue after
finishing a Book."*

—JOHN CHEEVER

I F YOU HAVE BEEN FOLLOWING YOUR BLUEPRINT FOR WRITING, BY now you have constructed your finished product—your script or manuscript. It's your calling card that shows you can write a properly structured, solid body of work.

Just as a model must have a portfolio and a singer a demo record, you the writer must have your finished product or products, that show you are a full-fledged writer.

Your finished product is your entree for selling your book or screenplay and is proof in black and white that you are a writer! You must make your work reflect the best writing you can do, so you'll be proud to show it around as representative of your writing talent and ability.

Even if it isn't bought by a producer or publisher to be made into a film or book, don't despair. Many writers have gotten assignments to write other projects after executives have read and were impressed with their writing ability.

No one will hire you if you don't have a sample of your writing to show. Everyone involved in the financial end of a project must be confident you know how to start, structure, and complete your work. They only gain that confidence by witnessing your ability to lay out the structure of your story, to create exciting characters, to motivate them, to write fresh dialogue, and to have a working knowledge of plotting a story from beginning to climax.

Suppose you are lucky and a director, producer, or star is interested in your work. If they like it, they could take it to the networks as a package deal, which means your script or manuscript would have a major star or director or production company attached as part of a package, making it more attractive to those in charge. This is especially true if the star, producer, or director has a commercial reputation.

When you enter the world of business, and this is the Writing Business, it's imperative to have some hard evidence of who you sent your project to and when. So keep records of each submission, who you submitted to, and the date. This gives you a time frame for making a follow-up call to check on the status of your work. In a worst-case scenario, your correspondence could serve as a paper trail if you ever felt your work was plagiarized or used without your permission.

You can also follow the same pattern with a novel. Nowadays, many film industry people are paying for options on best-selling novels, many of which are being made into feature films or miniseries for television. But getting a package deal is impossible without a finished script or manuscript, so let's focus on those qualities essential for a marketable story!

When you pick your subject matter for the story in your script, it's better to write a contemporary piece. Avoid the epic or period piece as they are costly and seldom made. By writing a novel you have a lot more freedom in your choice of subject matter, which is why historical romances and period pieces are so popular. Readers love experiencing the past and foreign places, so don't limit yourself if you're writing a novel—the sky's the limit.

Realize there are no new plots under the sun. All have been done over and over, but *not by you*. So go for a story that is uniquely yours. Write one that will be fresh and novel, featuring your own point of view. Make it a work of originality by writing what you know and by revealing who you are. Your personal involvement will make your story come alive. People will want to read more from a new writer whose voice makes a difference, that needs to be heard!

I have developed a checklist for my students to guide them when they are developing a project. It shows them all the necessary elements to include and the proper building blocks to use for great structure. Here are some guidelines for you to follow when writing your story. Keep the check list handy as you write and use it as your personal guide.

BLUEPRINT FOR WRITING

1. Do you have only one main character?

2. Does your main character have a desperate goal he wants to reach?

3. Did you write your ending first and then work backward to the beginning?

4. Does your opening set off the action of the story?

5. Is your main character active, not passive?

6. Do you have conflict in every scene and chapter?

7. Does every character in your work advance the main character's story?

8. Have the first ten pages hooked your audience or reader?

9. Does every scene or chapter relate to your plot structure or spine?

10. Does your work have a single storyline?

11. Are all your scenes written in a cause-and-effect manner? How do you know?

12. Is there an emotional relationship between your main character and another character? With whom?

13. Does your main character change in the climax?

14. Is your plot resolved in the climax?

15. Does each chapter or scene have a single purpose? Write it in a sentence or two.

16. Through whose point of view do you tell your story?

HOW TO SURVIVE THE WRITING GAME

"Henceforth I ask not good fortune.
I myself am good fortune."

—WALT WHITMAN

AT THE WRITER'S CENTER, I TEACH WRITERS TECHNIQUES FOR developing "one's emotional survival kit," career strategies, communication skills, how to present yourself, how to network, how to get recognition, and how to get people to listen to you and your ideas. When I get to this part of the workshop, writers are amazed at how little they know about the *business* aspect of writing.

This chapter includes the last component of the *Ballon*cing Method, dealing with your career and how to survive it. Since most writers have to sell themselves as well as their writing, they are at a definite advantage over the competition if they know some techniques to help them succeed in the writing game.

In the 1990s it's more difficult than ever to be a writer. Doing business is tough and only competitive and resourceful writers will survive. Publishing companies, networks, and movie studios are being bought by giant conglomerates and there are more executives interested in the bottom line than the creative line.

In no other business does an individual have to put himself on the line more than a writer every time he pitches an idea, writes a screenplay, produces a project, sends a query letter, or meets with a publisher. Yet nobody is less qualified to "do business" than writers. Why? Because writers spend most of their time mastering craft and none of it learning how to sell the results.

Writers study, go to workshops, perfect their craft, and when they finally write their project to the best of their ability, pouring their heart and soul into their writing, they're completely unprepared for the next step of the writing game: *They have to market themselves in an over-crowded marketplace, where the supply of talent greatly exceeds the demand.* Soon they discover paying their dues isn't enough, and that they have to deal with people who make decisions about their writing and their future, based not on the merit of the writing, but on many other variables. A single "yea" or "nay" can break a career or break a heart.

Through the past decade of witnessing some of the devastating effects of this business, I realized there were few resources available for writers who must constantly go into the marketplace, unprepared in the business and marketing skills they need to sell their writing. The fall-out of this constant "putting yourself on the line" creates self-doubt and low self-esteem.

Many writers have written wonderful books, scripts, sitcoms, short stories, plays, and children's books. Most of them, at first, have felt that just completing the writing was enough. In truth, it's only your ability to SELL your writing that allows you to survive in the writing game.

Producing a portfolio of writing is great, but that's only the first step. You must have a plan. Know who the decision makers are and how to reach them, rather than dealing with entry-level employees in the organizations you'd like to buy your writing. Too many beginners think all they have to do is finish writing and their work will sell. Some never do realize that the writing process includes writing and SELLING their script or manuscript.

You must be adept in both areas to be successful, becoming a salesperson who can convince other people what a terrific writer you are. You have to sell agents, producers, publishers, editors, and network executives on your idea and on you. Hate to sell? Wait a minute, you're selling all the time, wherever you go, whoever you meet, whatever you say. Remember, first you are selling yourself. What do you say about yourself before you say anything?

What self-image do you want to create when you sell your writing? Think about your clothing, your posture, your facial expression, your gestures, your hair, your eye contact, your hand-shake. You can plan in advance what image you wish to project. Projecting a positive self-image will help you sell your work. Your writing can be the most wonderful masterpiece in the world, but if you present a negative self-image as a writer you won't sell anything. You seldom get a second chance to make a first impression, so make yours a good one.

I have worked with many talented writers who were never able to sell their work. Not because they didn't know how to write, but because they didn't know how to TALK! You have to make it easy for people to want to listen to you. Preparation is the answer to getting listened to. Is there enthusiasm in your voice, are you excited about what you say? Are you credible in what you say and how you say it? Do you speak in a monotone, in a whisper, or so fast no one can understand you?

When you present your idea don't apologize, hesitate, or become embarrassed. Use a strong voice, direct eye contact, and speak clearly and confidently.

If you have to talk to an agent, editor, or producer on the telephone, it's often helpful to write out a script of what you want to say, practicing it until you sound as if you believe what you're saying.

Have you screenwriters, television writers, and dramatists mastered your three-sentence pitch?

What is your first sentence, your second sentence, your third? Write down the sentences and study your pitch. Have you gotten your listener's interest and attention? Does it sound exciting and focused?

Practice your pitch into a tape recorder before you have a meeting. Anticipate any questions or objections in advance so you can have answers prepared. Think of what kind of resistance you might encounter when you present your work and figure out how to overcome the resistance of others without becoming defensive. Remember, you're a professional writer and you need to reflect that image.

If when you're pitching your script an executive or editor makes suggestions or starts to change the focus, LET THEM! You *want* to get that person you're pitching to excited and involved in your script. So let them think it's their idea and keep quiet when they start talking. NEVER say, "I don't like your suggestion." or "That's not what I meant."

People in decision-making positions like to think their ideas are great, so don't tell them otherwise until they're sold on your script!

Unfortunately, I have seen many mediocre writers sell their writing while more talented writers can't. Unfair? Yes, but so is life. Many people have sold merely on the merits of their presentation and their ability to sell, not necessarily on the work itself.

Self-esteem is the key to success or failure in anything. Too many writers suffer from feelings of inadequacy, feeling "I am not enough," especially when it comes to selling themselves. Self-esteem is based on what you think and feel about yourself, not what someone else thinks and feels about you! You must have self-esteem, not only to keep you motivated when you're writing, but especially when you start selling your work. If you don't, the first rejection will put you into a tailspin and send you crashing into the depths.

Before you submit your writing you need a plan. Do some research on the companies you want to submit your script to. If you've written a science fiction script and your target production company or movie studio makes nothing but action/adventures, forget them, you won't stand a chance. If you've written a romance novel, don't bother to send your work to a publisher that only does horror fiction. You must study the market BEFORE you make your submissions. Target your script and your manuscript to a likely company.

If you get a rejection, don't take it personally! The last thing you should do is base your self-esteem on getting rejected or being accepted. *All a rejection means is that your product is not what the company is buying.* Don't try to project whether your work has merit or not. Just tell yourself you're not selling what they want to buy. File away the rejection while you put another manuscript into the mail. Many successful screenwriters never sold their first script until *after* they sold their third and fourth.

Don't sit around and wait for the phone to ring or the mail to come. Keep busy! Have some interests and a life outside your writing. Live your life as fully as you can while waiting for an answer. The best thing you can do is start another project and keep writing during the waiting period. Besides, you need a body of work, so now is the time to be productive. Do not sit around and wait. If you can afford it, this would be a good time to get away to germinate some ideas for your next project. Nothing improves your creative spirit than being relaxed, unstressed, and out of the pressure cooker. So go for some R & R.

All along I have been telling you to write from your heart and from your life experiences. Now, you must do the *opposite.* This is the time to remove yourself emotionally from your writing. Treat it as a product you're trying to sell. This is easier said than done, but it's necessary.

Look at your product with an objective writer's eye and cut your personal attachment. Sure you're going to feel depressed if you're rejected, but you can't let that get you down. Your motivation to sell your script must be internal and come from you. Your desire to produce and sell your writing must be *your* goal, not one you want for someone else. Your writing ability can't depend on whether someone in "BCA Company" rejected your script.

Always have your script "out there." Continue to send it out no matter what happens. If you haven't heard after a reasonable amount of time, follow up with a phone call or a personal letter. Many times I have had to call or write a letter to find out the status of a script after I had sent it out to production companies, studios, and agents.

Obviously, your script or manuscript is not the only one they are considering, but it certainly is the only one you're interested in. So, it's up to you to follow up if you don't know its status. Even if your writing is rejected by everyone you've sent it to, find some more places to send it. Failure is not being rejected. Failure is giving up trying. Who's to say your next submission won't be the one that sells!

In the writing game, you must have an unswerving belief in yourself and in your work. On the other hand, you must be flexible enough to make changes in your script or book or play when they're warranted. Don't wear blinders or let your ego take over your better judgment. If you hear the same criticism again and again, listen to it and do the necessary rewriting. If you're not certain what to do, hire a script or writing consultant! But when you feel your product is absolutely the best it will ever be, stick to your guns and be firm.

When I wrote my first non-fiction book, I got a call from an agent in New York who wanted to represent me. She started telling me what changes she wanted me to make in the manuscript. Since she was my first agent, I was ready to rewrite the entire book. Lucky for me, I spoke with an experienced writer who told me, "Don't make any changes for this agent until she finds a publisher who wants you to sign a contract, then tell her you'll be happy to make any changes they want."

I was afraid to take that advice, but I did. And you know what? The agent took me on as a client without my changing a single word. Nevertheless, since then, I have made changes when I felt an agent's criticism about my writing was absolutely right. So use your intuition, your good judgment, and your faith in yourself and let your common sense tell you what to do.

The writing game is difficult enough to play. If you want to win, don't sabotage yourself. In other words "Don't stab yourself in the back." Take good care of yourself, eat properly, exercise, have friends and interests other than writing, do charity work, and have a life besides writing.

Take a course in marketing or selling. If you get too depressed and it affects your entire life, get help from a professional therapist. In any situation where you are the creator of your product it is difficult to sustain your motivation if you're always depressed and feeling hopeless.

Wishing, hoping, praying, or just working hard isn't enough to gain you the professional recognition you want. First you must decide what you want to write, then you target the publishing companies, magazines, studios, or networks. Next, YOU have to create a plan to reach your goals, whatever they are. Don't wait for others to do it for you, and that even includes those of you who have an agent. Ultimately, it's up to you to get what you want for yourself.

How can you sell me on you and your writing abilities, if you're embarrassed to tell me all the good things about yourself? Create a "brag sheet" listing all your attributes as a writer and as a person. Put down everything you've written, your credits, your resumé—all the projects you want to write. Read your brag sheet over every day and every night until you start to believe you have credibility.

Do you hear an inner voice saying, "It's not nice to brag"? Don't listen to that voice anymore! And what's the matter with saying good things about yourself to other people? You sure don't have a problem saying negative things, do you?

People believe what you say about yourself, so start listening to all the negative things you tell everyone. Change the things you say to positives. Just for practice, team up with another writer and spend five minutes telling him what a terrific writer you are and how excited you are about your latest writing project. How did you do? That wasn't too hard, was it? How did you feel saying nice things about yourself? My guess is it wasn't easy for you. Ask your friend to give you honest feedback on how convincing you sounded. Work on improving those things you need to improve. Practice does make perfect, and that goes for saying good things about yourself, too. So practice answering positively whenever someone says, "Hi, how are you doing?"

"Great, I'm so excited about the (fill in the blank) I just finished. I can't wait to get it into the marketplace."

This attitude will create a positive reaction in other people about you and your work, so the next time they see you they'll remember you're doing well.

People want to associate with winners. And in the writing game, you certainly want to present yourself as a winner, even if you've never sold anything. How can anyone have the confidence to put large sums of money into your project if you don't believe in it? Now's the time to begin creating a winning image of yourself as a writer.

Which leads me to one of the most pervasive problems writers have. Answer this question. "Do you take yourself seriously as a writer?" Think about it before you answer. Can you introduce yourself as a writer? If not, why? Can you think of yourself as a writer? If not, why?

Your winning attitude begins with you. Right now—start to TAKE YOURSELF SERIOUSLY AS A WRITER! If you don't, I won't and neither will agents or producers, network and studio executives, or publishers to whom you're trying to sell your script or manuscript.

Successful writers don't live in fear and they aren't afraid to make mistakes and take risks when their work is rejected. That's when they stay committed to their work, until they find someone who likes it. Professionals remain passionate about their writing and never give up.

Why is it we always use our negative self-talk to put ourselves down for being rejected, instead of praising ourselves for taking a risk over and over and over again, by constantly and consistently sending out our work?

How would you treat another writer if she got rejected? What would you tell her? Probably something along the lines of: "Don't put yourself down." "It's the work that got rejected, not you." "Dr. Seuss was rejected over 56 times before his first book was published." "They don't know good writing when they see it."

But what do you say to yourself? I guarantee you aren't that kind or gentle to yourself. Well, now is the time to nurture yourself just like you do others. You need to recognize how much negative programming you have built in and deliberately counteract it if you are rejected. Write down positive affirmations about yourself and your work and read them over, especially after a rejection.

Above all, don't lose confidence or belief in yourself and your writing, especially if you feel you've given it 100 percent. Look at any criticism not through your ego, but with a professional writer's objectivity. Be professional enough to let go of things that don't work and to change your material for the better even if it means rewriting an entire book or script. But remember, at some point, you must believe in your work no matter what! If you don't, you'll constantly be affected badly by every rejection until you'll find yourself unable to write.

Your motivation for writing can't come from anyone else, it must come from inside you. When you're rejected, go back and review your reasons for wanting to be a writer in the first place. Don't let any person or any outside circumstances keep you from achieving your goal. Because without that internal belief and trust in yourself and your work, you'll never make it as a writer. You must continue to send your work out week after week without giving up or getting down.

Every writer gets rejected, so having a community of writers to talk to and pour out your heart to is essential. Find other writers to meet with and develop a support system or writers network, especially when you're dealing with marketing frustrations and rejection. Writers need all the support they can get and in my Writer's Support Groups we give emotional support, career support, and craft support. We deal with personal and professional issues like writer's block, rejection, and overcoming procrastination. I also coach writers on how to play the writing game, giving them techniques and strategies on how to speak and act on interviews, at pitch meetings, and over the telephone.

These skills are vital for writers in the entertainment industry who constantly have to pitch their ideas. There is no other industry as dysfunctional as the entertainment industry. I've seen talented writers with fabulous scripts get rejected and writers who couldn't write at all given hundreds of thousands of dollars for a script, only to have a studio hire someone else to rewrite it.

By now you have learned how to successfully play the writing game by the rules. Speaking of rules, I have found that sometimes ignorance really is bliss. A few years ago, two writers from another state came to Los Angeles to meet with me about their script. They arrived a day early so they could visit agents, and since they didn't know the rules, made a list of addresses of some agents whom they wanted to represent them. They didn't even call, but went directly to the agents' offices and said they wanted a meeting. Do you know what? They got one. Of course, it was on the merits of their script, but on the other hand, if they knew the rules they would NEVER have barged into agents' offices without an appointment or a personal referral.

Okay, so after you know the rules, sometimes you need to break them. What better way to get an appointment or meeting with a producer, an agent, or a studio executive, than to be creatively outrageous or unique in your approach. Let your imagination soar and find original ways to make yourself visible.

In the writing game, criticism always seems easier to give than praise, and everyone is a Monday morning quarterback. People in entertainment or publishing are constantly telling writers what's *not* working in their script or manuscript. The balance between criticism and writing is difficult for many writers to maintain, because they allow themselves to be affected by the whims and wiles of too many other people who often make their decisions not on the merits of a script or manuscript, but based on their own subjectivity, ego needs, and insecurities.

Unfortunately, some people who give advice (solicited or not), who can even okay a project, often have little or no knowledge of craft. In fact, some people keep their jobs, especially in the entertainment industry, by always saying "no," since that seems safer than putting themselves on the line and having a script turn out to be a flop or a financial disaster like *Howard the Duck*.

Recently a writer asked me what to do about his agent. This agent, with a reputable firm, liked a screenplay my client wrote and decided to represent him. But my client's calls weren't returned and the agent's secretary always had excuses for her boss (he was on the phone, in a meeting, out to lunch, out of town, out of the office, etc.) When my client asked for his script back, he discovered that, after having it one year, the agent had sent it out to only five production companies. "I was so frustrated when I discovered it was only sent to five production companies in a year," he said. "Now, I have to start the process of getting an agent all over again."

Many writers don't know what to expect from an agent, since most are just thrilled even to get one in the first place. As in any business, you have to know the individuals you're dealing with and in the writing business, you have to learn what works best with your particular agent and what doesn't. Did you notice I used the word "business?" That's because getting an agent and dealing with one is business and it's important for you to approach it as such.

Try to form a partnership with your agent and to develop a rapport. Get to know your agent's taste, so he will be excited with your work, because if your agent doesn't believe in your script, chances are it won't be sold.

Even though it's difficult to get an agent, in truth, after you sign the contract, an agent works for you and is YOUR employee. Sound strange? You probably can't even think in those terms, you are so thrilled just to have an agent. It all goes back to the law of supply and demand, and in this business, the demand for agents far exceeds the supply.

Here are a few strategies I suggest to writers for dealing with their agents:

First, rather than being afraid to call or sitting back and waiting for something to happen, we worked out a specific plan for them to be active in their own career. Rather than calling with an "I hope I'm not being a pest," attitude or "Have you heard from anyone, yet?" they called with specific information to help their agent like, "I ran into Bob Jones over at XYZ studio and he'd like you to send him my script."

This change of attitude helped them form a better relationship with their agent. The writers began to feel more in control of their careers and the agents began to have more respect for them.

Recently, I invited an agent to speak at the Writer's Center. She made some wonderful points that I would like to share with you.

She told the group she had only so much time during the course of the day, and she had to spread it out among a lot of writers. She asked the following question: "If I work with over fifty clients, and I'm trying to sell each one's work in only so much time, the question is: 'Who do you think your career is more important to—me or you? Do you get the message? It's up to you to do as much work as you can, to help your agent sell you and your writing. That means you must be active in trying to meet people in the business, you need to network (whether you like to or not) and you need to tell people what a terrific writer you are. You never know if the person next to you in line at the bank couldn't be someone looking for a script or novel!"

This agent went on to say she likes a client who is prolific and who keeps writing new projects NO MATTER WHAT! This means if your last screenplay was rejected, you don't give up, you keep on creating new product. Most agents like clients who bring them new sample sitcoms or hour episodes, or teleplays, or whatever genre you want to write for. They don't want you to just sit back and wait for that one script or manuscript to sell. Agents want their clients to have a body of work they can use to show off their talents. The more product they have to sell, the easier the agent's job.

If you feel your relationship with your agent is like a bad marriage, get out. Don't waste your time and energy trying to make it better, because you probably can't. Agents like to deal with writers who are enthusiastic and confident about themselves and their work. It makes the selling of both much easier, when a client can be personable and successfully handle a pitch meeting after the agent sets one up.

As in any relationship, you must have give and take. Most important of all is mutual respect. You should be able to sit down with your agent and help plan strategies to sell your work and further your career. Your relationship with your agent should be a partnership, both of you having the same goal—your writing success.

By taking an active part in your career, being responsible for initiating new contacts, developing new writing products, and believing in yourself and your writing, you will help your agent achieve success for you. Then you will be a major player who will win the writing game!

Stick with your game plan and do the best writing you know how, use your personal vision and truth and reach deep inside to put yourself into your script. One day someone will recognize your ability and talent, but in the meantime you need to keep writing, keep sending out your work, and keep your writing goals in mind. You'll win the writing game if you're willing to improve your skills and master your craft, market yourself from the inside out, and above all to be persistent. Keep on writing, no matter what, and you'll not only survive, you'll thrive at playing the writing game.

BLUEPRINT FOR WRITING

1. Why aren't good screenplays enough?

2. What's the worst part about getting rejected?

3. Why do you need a market approach to your writing?

4. What are you selling? Who are you selling to?

5. What does your product look like?

6. What do you want to write? In what format?

7. What market are you selling to? What do they need? Does your writing fit those needs?

8. Practice writing a three-sentence "pitch."
   A. *What's in the first sentence?*
   B. *What's in the second sentence?*
   C. *What's in the third sentence?*
   D. *Deliver your three-sentence pitch to others.*
   E. *Check for clarity and focus. Get feedback.*

9. What do you say about yourself before you say anything?

10. Write how others would describe you.

11. Write about what you want them to say.

12. What happens when you open your mouth?

13. How do you introduce yourself?

14. How do you talk about your writing?

15. Create a Brag Sheet. List all your credits, your writing ability, your talent.

16. List reasons why you take yourself seriously as a writer.

17. Always introduce yourself as a writer.

18. Tell another person about your work.

19. List everyone you've ever met who could help you in the writing game.

20. List five ways you can make more contacts.

21. What do you do if you don't have an agent?

22. How do you get an agent?

23. What do you do when your work is rejected?

24. What happens after you get rejected?

25. What are some personal barriers that might hold you back?

26. Develop a workable plan for surviving the writing game.

THE WRITER'S PATH

"Writing is making sense of life."

—NADINE GORDIMER

W RITING IS ABOUT THE MOST PERSONAL CRAFT ANY ARTIST can practice. It is always difficult for other people to separate the writing from the writer. If a writer is depressed, feeling blocked, or angry, it is often reflected in his writing. On the other hand, a musician can be angry and still play his instrument, and a dancer can be depressed and still dance.

In my opinion, a writer is the one artist whose craft is most directly connected to his emotions and feelings. And often a writer's feelings can create considerable pain, especially when it involves writing.

It is very difficult for a writer to separate herself from her work when it is rejected. After all, she has written from her heart, about her values, her life experiences, her beliefs, her passions, from her soul. How can she not take this rejection personally?

But she must not take it personally, and she must keep on working in the face of rejection and disappointment!

A writer must be motivated enough to continue to write after he has been rejected again and again. This is difficult enough, especially when he must continue to write and has no guarantee that after finishing, anyone will even be interested in his work.

Given these harsh realities, now that you have completed your *Blueprint for Writing*, do you still want to be a writer? Have your motives for becoming a writer changed after all the time, effort, and hard work you've put into completing your writing project?

Do you still want success? Do you still want to be rich and famous? Or must you write about your beliefs, hopes, and burning desires, and share your vision with the world? If the answer to the last question is "yes," you must continue with the writing game and don't stop until you win.

Many talented writers in my workshops have read their work in class and mesmerized everyone. Unfortunately, most will never finish a novel or a script, because they won't put in the long hours and do the hard work it takes to complete a work.

It's fairly easy to write a scene or a vignette, but try putting together scene after scene or chapter after chapter into a successful script or novel. That's hard work and only the most committed writers will succeed. A long time ago, I discovered that talent is a great gift, but it's hard work and the desire to complete a body of work that produces writing success.

A few years ago, a lawyer attended my writing workshop. He was NOT the most talented writer. In fact, some of his work was stilted and rigid because he was so used to writing law briefs. But he was clear and concise, although his writing lacked passion.

After he completed the beginning workshop, he joined my advanced workshop with about ten other people. Guess what? Of all the talented people in that class the lawyer is the only one who has a body of work. Why? Because he wasn't afraid of the hard work entailed in writing a novel. He used the same skills as in his law practice that allowed him the financial security to retire in his late forties and devote his time to becoming a writer: discipline, creating a schedule and sticking to it, never giving up when blocked but continuing to write, and setting daily, weekly, and yearly writing goals. In other words, he had a destination or a goal for his writing. It worked! He completed his novel and is working on his second.

It takes more than talent to succeed as a writer. It takes hard work, goal setting, but most of all it takes PERSEVERANCE and CONSISTENCY to win the writing game.

Too many writers want results without paying their dues, without making enough of an effort. They are not dedicated writers, they only want to be called "writers" without doing the work.

I am amazed how many people think that if they can write a sentence or a good personal letter they are writers. Would any of you presume to think yourselves a professional ice skater or concert pianist just because you took a few lessons? Would you try to join the Ice Capades as a professional skater or decide to give a piano recital because you could play a few songs on the piano? Of course not. The same holds true with writing.

Sometimes writers feel guilty because they don't automatically have a great desire to wake up and rush to their computer or typewriter. They think they're not writers because they feel they *should* love the work and they don't. Others wonder why they must STRUGGLE like they do until they get into their writing.

The reason for all this is quite logical. *Writing is hard work!* There's no getting around that: it takes concentration, discipline, creative energy, and motivation to face an empty page and know you have to create something from nothing. Besides your creativity, there is the daily struggle with the work itself. Is your structure solid? Does the story flow? Is your main character exciting and credible? Does your plot create tension and suspense?

HOW TO MAKE YOURSELF A PRODUCTIVE WRITER

Are you willing to master your craft? Do you want to learn the rules? Are you willing to put in a year or two of your life or more to write your manuscript or script? Does your desire to write come from the inside, so you'll continue no matter what? If it does, then here are some things you should do to make yourself a productive writer.

Always work hard and be consistent. Take life as you see it and through your writing bring some meaning to it. Make your point of view heard and try to move your audience emotionally with your writing. Keep your goal in sight and keep working towards it, especially when you feel like quitting.

Have the courage and perseverance to fight for your work when it's not succeeding exactly as you want it to. Be resilient and flexible. Never give up! Stick with it until you make it work!

You can succeed as a writer if you are willing to write and write and write. Writing is really rewriting. Rewriting will make your work better and better. Work steadily and be persistent. Writing is not thinking about writing or talking about writing or reading books on writing. Writing is writing. Just keep writing!

Writing is a habit and it takes practice to develop better habits. Although I don't mean to sound rigid, I think you need to set a schedule for yourself and follow it religiously. Otherwise, if you don't practice your craft you won't improve it. Write every day, even if only for fifteen to thirty minutes. Don't feel guilty if you can't write, that is a waste of energy, but do try to be consistent.

Consistency is another way to master your craft and improve your writing. All the talent in the world counts for little if you have no knowledge of craft. Writing *is* a craft, so it takes repetition and practice; as with any other skill, practice makes perfect. So pump up your writing muscles. Your art will come from perfecting the craft, combining that with your passion and honesty when telling your story.

Develop an idea file. Keep a notebook with you at all times to record dreams, conversations, conflicts, and personal experiences. Be an observer of human nature and behavior and learn to probe the inner depths by looking behind the masks of other people.

Experience life by participating. Expect to make mistakes, but learn from them. Those who succeed in the writing game take failure and turn it into success by never giving up and by working over and over despite momentary setbacks.

Think of preparing to be a writer as an athlete would train to compete. Successful athletes have a goal in sight, never wavering from it, no matter what the obstacles. They practice every day, mastering their craft until they're perfect!

If, as a writer, you could apply the same determination as those winning athletes, mirroring their dedication, and their singleness of purpose, and be willing to devote just as much time and energy to mastering your craft as they do perfecting their sport, you will certainly become a winning writer.

By finishing this book, you are well on your way to writing a film script, novel, television show, play, or sitcom. You have your own *Blueprint for Writing* now, so you can't get sidetracked or lost along the way. If you work this book and master its techniques of structure and character development, I assure you that eventually you will get work.

The writing game has just begun for you. Good luck and good writing and you will surely win the game.

FOR INFORMATION ON
RACHEL BALLON'S WRITER'S CENTER
OR TO INQUIRE ABOUT
INDIVIDUAL CONSULTATIONS OR WORKSHOPS
CALL (310) 479-0048

OR WRITE TO:
P.O. BOX 491414
LOS ANGELES, CA. 90049

HIT OR MISS

BY RACHEL BALLON & ADRIENNE FAYNE

A crying woman rushes down a corridor to a door with the name "NORMAN SHORTMAN M.D., Plastic Surgeon—Reconstructive Surgery, A Medical Corporation" on it in black letters. She opens the door and enters the waiting room, filled with patients who have recently had plastic or cosmetic surgery. One woman has two black eyes and a partially bandaged nose. One man has a huge bandage around his face. A woman with swollen eyes is sitting alone. CHARLENE PATTERSON, early 30s, walks to the receptionist and continues crying as she talks.

The receptionist picks up the phone and buzzes DR. NORMAN SHORTMAN, 45, slightly balding, attractive. He is in an examining room kissing his office manager, LISA WHITNEY, 29, blond and beautiful. The receptionist tells him he's urgently needed to see Ms. Patterson, as she is creating a disturbance in the office. Lisa begins to argue and tells him she can't take any more sneaking around. She gives him an ultimatum: He has to leave his wife in six months or she's never going to see him again. He promises her he'll do it, but she has to understand he doesn't want to hurt his wife, Brenda. She has been a loving wife and mother for twenty-five years and she's never been on her own.

Lisa asks Norman what he intends to do and he tells her it would probably be better to get Brenda to leave him. If only she'd find someone to have an affair with, it wouldn't be so hard on her when he left.

Lisa laughs and tells him she thinks that's not a very good possibility—after all, has he taken a good look at his wife recently? She's sweet and wonderful but nothing great to look at. Norman decides maybe he should do some cosmetic surgery on Brenda like he did for Lisa.

The receptionist buzzes again and tells him to hurry, his patient is getting hysterical. Lisa tells him he had better calm down his patient, since he can't afford another malpractice suit.

He enters the room where Charlene Patterson is sitting and crying. Her operation didn't work. Norman tells her not to worry, because he'll fix everything, all he needs to do is take a tuck or two. He continues to charm and soothe her until she calms down and finally smiles at him, telling him she's sorry for being upset. Norman takes advantage of the moment and tries to talk her into having a facelift. She agrees.

The next morning Norman is having breakfast with his wife, BRENDA SHORTMAN, 42, attractive but matronly. He tells her he doesn't understand why she stays married to him, since he's always working and never home. She says how much she loves him and that she keeps busy gardening, playing tennis, and reading murder mysteries.

In fact, she's going to a lecture today by some of her favorite mystery writers. He continues telling her he knows he's not a very good husband, and she'd be better off without him, since she's in her prime—the kids are grown and he's always leaving her alone. She kisses him and tells him not to worry, she only has eyes for him.

As Brenda is about to leave, the mail comes and a brochure arrives advertising a 7-day cruise for health practitioners. Brenda suggests Norman and she sign up for it—it would be good for him to get away from all of his lawsuits, patients, and work. Feeling guilty, Norman tells her okay.

Brenda is in the audience at a local community center, where KEN BARRETT, 39, dark haired and artsy, is one of the featured writers. He and the other writers are behind a curtain waiting to be introduced. He wears a tweed jacket with suede patches at the elbows and talks to his literary agent, MAX ZIMMERMAN, 52. They argue about Ken spending all of the advance from his forthcoming book and not writing the first hundred pages. His publishers are furious and want either the material or their money back immediately.

Max tells Ken he's going to lose everything if he doesn't start producing some work. Ken doesn't seem too worried, everything except his typewriter is rented anyway, and nobody's going to take that. Max shakes his head and tells him to lay off the booze, because he has to speak in a couple of minutes and all of his fans are waiting to hear him.

The audience is clapping after the speeches. Afterwards, as Ken mingles with the audience, Brenda shyly edges over to Ken and tells him how she loves his writing and that he has so much feeling in his characterizations. The two hit it off and she asks him when his next mystery is coming out. He abruptly changes the subject and is saved by other fans crowding around him.

That night Norman is playing poker with five other doctors who meet for a weekly game. One of the regulars is sick and DR. LEON GOLDNER is filling in. He's complaining that he really shouldn't be playing since he doesn't have any money. The others joke and say he's loaded, like all dermatologists. He explains that he thought he was going to get a short, simple divorce from his wife of ten years, but instead it's been a year of lawyers, accountants, tax experts, appraisers, and misery. His wife ended up with a killer for an attorney and they took him to the cleaners. He tells the men if he had it to do over he'd probate rather than litigate.

Norman is visibly upset when he hears Leon telling the group that he's in debt up to his transplanted hair. What is he going to do now? Brenda helped put him through medical school working as a secretary. And he recently put his investments in her name to avoid personal liability since he's being sued by disgruntled patients. He is shaken up by the conversation and as he gets up to leave hears Leon asking the others if they know any available men to fix his ex up with. He's desperate to get her married, because he wouldn't have to pay any more alimony.

Norman decides he must fix up his own wife and get her interested in another man. It will be impossible to get divorced if what Leon says is true. He decides to go to the best divorce attorney in town to find out himself.

When he arrives home Brenda is waiting up. She makes several amorous attempts to seduce him, but he complains about being tired from all the problems he's encountering in his practice and with the various lawsuits.

He tells Brenda he needs some understanding from her. He turns and studies her face telling her it wouldn't hurt to get her eyes and face done. She says a few wrinkles don't upset her, besides she's earned them. He tells her he's working late again tomorrow night at the private hospital and won't be home until three or four in the morning and not to wait up. She's disappointed and doesn't understand what kind of hospital wants doctors to work those hours. He becomes defensive and says he already explained he deals with working people who have regular work hours and if she doesn't trust him maybe she should find another husband.

Brenda quickly apologizes and tells him about the wonderful day she had meeting her favorite mystery writer, Ken Barrett. Norman is already snoring.

Norman makes an appointment and visits a lawyer, whose office is filled with antiques and plush velvet furniture. There is a wet bar off to one side and a personal valet offers Norman a drink. While Norman is looking around the office a door opens and MARLIN FINKMAN enters, 50ish, naked except for a towel wrapped around his waist, smoking a cigar. He introduces himself, apologizing for being late, but his massage and steam took longer than he expected. He takes a drink from his valet and sits down behind a massive antique desk, towel and all. He begins to ask Norman questions about his financial status and the value of his practice, in between talking to his stockbroker, his real estate manager, and his financial consultant.

After Norman tells the attorney that his wife put him through medical school, the lawyer tells him he'll have to split his medical practice with her. Norman is beside himself. When he tells Marlin about all of his financial problems and his lack of assets, the attorney immediately becomes disinterested and declines to take him on as a client, telling him he'd be better off with a less expensive lawyer, and in fact he'd be better off not getting divorced.

All of Norman's fears are confirmed. In fact, he realizes not only would a divorce be too expensive, but so would the lawyer handling it.

Norman is at Lisa's apartment very upset. He tells her about the visit to the attorney and that he is desperate to find a husband for his wife, or Lisa and he will have a lot of money problems because he has to split everything with his wife including his practice. Lisa becomes angry and tells him she has no intention of working all her life, she's entitled to more than that after all the time she's wasted with him. He tries to kiss her but she resists until he placates her by taking a velvet black box from his jacket pocket. He hands her a diamond watch and Lisa thanks him by giving him a passionate kiss. Lisa says she hates to add to his problems, but his insurance company called today and they are cancelling his malpractice insurance because of all his lawsuits. He is more desperate then ever to find a man for Brenda.

Norman comes up with the idea that he should throw a big party and invite all the single men he knows, then maybe Brenda can meet someone. Lisa suggests Brenda needs to be overhauled to get a man to notice her. No one will look at her unless she loses weight, gets her hair styled, and buys some fashionable clothes. After all, Brenda is no longer a young woman. He tells Lisa to pick out a sexy dress for Brenda to wear for the upcoming party.

Norman and Brenda are at a restaurant having dinner. He tells her he thinks they need to throw a big party, since they haven't entertained in a long time. He thinks it will bring in some new business and with the expenses he's been having he needs the business. He also wants to meet some people in the community and pay back a lot of associates so he can get more referrals. He stares at Brenda and tells her she's putting on weight and she should do something about her hair, like dye the gray.

Brenda is having a day at an Elizabeth Arden-type salon, where she is getting the entire beauty treatment, color, cut, style, and makeup. She is with her divorced girlfriend, ELAINE GOLDNER, middle 40s, attractive. The two are seated under the dryers talking. She tells Elaine she's thrilled that Norman's starting to pay so much attention to her. In fact, he even wants to throw a big party for their friends and business associates.

Elaine looks at her suspiciously and says Leon did that very same thing before he left her for another woman. Brenda gets insulted, but the seed is planted and she looks worried.

A week later Brenda and Norman are dressing for the party. The downstairs is filled with guests—mostly single doctors. Brenda looks out of place and uncomfortable with the way she's dressed. She keeps going into the kitchen to help the caterers and Norman gets angry because he wants her to meet all the eligible men at the party. Norman finds her in the kitchen and makes her come out to the party where he introduces her to all the available men. He brags to them about her abilities as a cook, tennis player, a terrific cleaner, and a loyal person. Brenda is mortified by his bragging and the men look at him like he's nuts. But it doesn't work. They aren't interested. And all of them eventually gravitate to Lisa, who is the center of attention with her gorgeous figure shown off by the sexy black see-through outfit Norman bought her. He becomes very jealous when he sees Lisa talking to BOB LEWIS, early 30s, a handsome young bachelor and the hottest plastic surgeon in town. He has taken a lot of the business away from Norman and others.

Bob and Lisa dance, drink, and talk all evening as Norman gets more jealous by the minute. Brenda walks into the library and accidentally overhears Norman confronting Lisa about her flirting with Bob Lewis. Brenda doesn't know for certain whether or not this is strictly business or if there's more to it. But the incident adds fuel to her suspicions and fears about her husband's fidelity or lack of it.

The last guest has left and Brenda is cleaning up after the party. She's upset about all the attention Norman gave to Lisa. Norman is just sitting in a chair looking into space. He isn't helping her clean up. She asks him what's the matter with him because he's looking so depressed. He says he is depressed. Why didn't she talk more to the men? Why couldn't she have been thinner, younger, more fun? Why did she stay in the kitchen half the night after he paid for a caterer?

Brenda gets upset and tells him she doesn't like the way he's acting. He ignored most of the guests and paid too much attention to a few of the others. Was something bothering him since he acted so rude? Still fishing for information Brenda says Lisa must help his practice since she gets along so well with everyone, and she's so young and pretty. She especially noticed how interested Bob Lewis seems to be in her and they make an adorable couple.

Norman explodes, saying that's ridiculous. Lisa can get her own dates, besides Bob Lewis is a phony, hack surgeon. He exits to the kitchen and slams the door behind him. Brenda's suspicions are stronger than ever.

Brenda is at a fashionable restaurant having lunch with Elaine. Elaine tells Brenda she's looking terrific, what could be so wrong? Brenda says she may have been right about Norman cheating on her and explains that he comes home late almost every night, and he's buying her presents he never bought in all their years of marriage. Elaine tells Brenda whatever you do, DON'T GET DIVORCED and STAY MARRIED! Elaine tells her she would have been better off with a criminal attorney than a divorce attorney.

Norman's in his office after hours and Lisa walks in. She looks terrific and asks Norman if he had any success finding a husband for Brenda. He tells her he didn't and he's sorry to disappoint her. He then says he can't go out tonight because he promised Brenda he'd be home for dinner, since she was so upset after the party. Lisa says she was going to have to break their date anyway, since she promised to help Bob Lewis set up his new filing system. Norman gets upset and Lisa says he's not her husband yet. Besides, it's strictly business. Norman tells her he'll call his wife and break their arrangements, but she's to cancel her appointment with Bob. Lisa refuses and says that would look unprofessional. Norman is terribly upset, they argue, and instead of going home, he goes to a bar.

Ken Barrett is sitting at the bar with a bottle in front of him. He's talking to his agent, Max, who tells him Ken's time is up and he must pay back the advance. He hasn't given the publishers the first hundred pages of his manuscript. Ken doesn't react because he's getting drunk. He's not even writing because he's suffering from acute writer's block and hasn't been able to write one page of his new book for the past three months. Max warns him about the seriousness of the situation—they're going to sue him and he's in big trouble. They argue and Max gets up to leave just as Norman walks in.

Norman is very depressed and goes to the bar and sits down next to Ken. He overhears Max yell something about if you don't finish the job by this week you'll have to pay back the advance or they'll go after you.

Norman is intrigued—he thinks they're talking about something illegal having to do with the mob. Curious, he offers to buy Ken a drink and tells him he couldn't help overhearing his argument and isn't life tough? He has problems too—maybe not life and death ones like Ken's, but big enough. After a couple of drinks together, Ken asks Norman about his problems. Norman tells him about his girl-friend, who is going out with another doctor tonight, and how upset Norman's been because he can't afford a divorce.

Ken listens to all the details and becomes more intrigued. Maybe he'll find some material for his new book. Ken, completely drunk, is sympathizing with Norman's plight, when almost absently he says Norman would be better off if she were dead!

Norman reacts. By God, he's right! After all, didn't Leon tell him only lawyers get rich during a divorce? And if he has no money he knows Lisa will never agree to marry him. Besides, he's batted zero trying to find Brenda a man. Thinking Ken is a hit man offering to do the job, Norman asks, "How much do you get?"

Ken misunderstands. He thinks Norman is talking about his advance and tells him it depends on how fast they want the job done as to how much they give him up front. Norman keeps questioning Ken until he discovers Ken's usual price is a $50,000 advance, $25,000 up front, the rest when the job is done.

Norman, still thinking Ken's with the mob, asks Ken who he works for and Ken tells him he is self-employed. Finally, Norman gets up his courage and in a conspiratorial voice tells Ken he'd like him to do a job for him. Ken is confused until Norman says, "I never dreamed I'd be asking a 'hit man' to kill my wife."

Ken chokes on his drink and starts to tell Norman he's made a mistake, until Norman takes out a wad of bills and peels off a thousand dollars, saying that's to seal the deal until he can get to his safe for the other $24,000.

Ken goes along with Norman and tells him he's not sure whether he'll do it, but if he decides to take the job he only deals in cash. It would take a lot of time, energy, and effort because when he does a job no one ever suspects it was anything but an accident.

Ken is really getting into the role. He takes out a laundry ticket and gives it to Norman, telling him if he decides to take the job he can put the $24,000 into a pair of socks and put them both inside a laundry bag with some clean shirts, along with a schedule of his wife's activities. He would have to have time to get to know everything about Norman's wife: studying her routine and getting to know it if he decides to take the job.

Norman gives Ken his card and tells him to think about it, but to call him only on his private line if he decides to take the job. The two shake hands and Norman staggers out of the bar.

Ken claps his hands and is delighted that he now has money and a story, too.

A few days later Norman gets a call from Ken, who has decided to do the job. He gives the address of the Chinese laundry on Matson street, tells Norman to meet him there, and be sure he has $24,000 in small bills.

Norman hesitates for a moment, but just then Lisa walks by and blows him a kiss. He gets back his resolve and tells Ken he'll have it the next morning. Ken tells him to come early, and that from this moment on they'll make contact only by phone. Norman is never to call him, but to wait for Ken's calls. Norman agrees, promising to deliver the goods the next morning.

Ken is waiting around the corner from the Chinese laundry and he has a full view of the front door. Both Norman and Ken wear the exact same outfit, beige raincoats and brimmed felt spy hats. Once Norman is out of sight, Ken enters the laundry.

The owners, MR. AND MRS. CHIN, ask Ken about the strange man who just dropped off a package for him, and ask whether he is in trouble. They offer to loan him some more money to pay his rent, but Ken tells them it isn't necessary. In fact, he's going to pay them back all the money he owes them right now. They look puzzled when he reaches into the just-delivered package and pulls out cash.

Ken asks for some strong cleaning fluid to get rid of a spot on his couch and they caution him to be careful because it's very flammable. Ken leaves with his shirts, his money, and the fluid.

Back at his apartment, he starts to experiment with the cleaning fluid, trying to make a bomb. He mixes the fluid with some other ingredients and the mixture starts to foam, running down his table onto the rug. The rug becomes burned and discolored. Then he takes a rope and tries to make a noose, but gets tangled up in the rope. There is a knock at the door—it's Ken's manager, Max. He sees the rope and tells Ken he came to give him some bad news, but thinking Ken may be suicidal, hesitates telling him.

Ken assures him he can handle the news and Max says his time limit is up and he has to pay back the advance today. Ken tells him he has the money and wants out of the deal, anyway.

Max is shocked and tells Ken he thinks it's time he took a vacation. He'll even lend him the money. Ken laughs, and says after Max left the bar last night he got a dynamite idea for a book, a blockbuster best seller he's starting to work on immediately.

Ken will call him when he's done and Max will get his commission.

The agent is bewildered and hopes Ken isn't drinking too much. When Max leaves, Ken goes to his closet and takes out a game of "Clue." He picks up each weapon and studies it, jotting notes in a small notebook.

Lisa walks into Norman's office and apologizes affectionately for not seeing him last night. She reiterates that she doesn't want to become an "old maid" waiting for him to leave his wife. Norman starts to blurt out he loves her so much he's hired a hit man, but is interrupted by the phone ringing. Lisa informs Norman he has a disgruntled patient in one of the examining rooms and he'd better go see her.

Brenda enters a fashionable Beverly Hills store to do some shopping. Brenda's getting in shape for the cruise she is taking with Norman.

Norman is at his weekly poker game at Leon Goldner's apartment. The apartment is devoid of furniture except for the card table and chairs. Leon is shirtless, complaining about how he should have listened to the friends who warned him about losing everything if he got divorced. He apologizes for the lack of furniture, but explains that while he was napping the other day he awoke to an apartment full of women and his ex-wife taking out the furniture. Norman is more desperate than ever.

The next morning Norman leaves for work in his Mercedes 580 SL with the top down. Ken is hiding in the bushes across the street, and while waiting is attacked by a large doberman. The owner calls off the dog and yells at Ken for snooping around their house. Ken picks himself up, his shirt ripped, pants torn, and binoculars broken, just in time to see Brenda drive off in her tennis clothes. He looks at the picture Norman gave him of Brenda and is surprised to see how different she looks from when he met her at the lecture.

The following day Ken waits for Brenda to leave the house, but this time he's in his car. The same dog jumps on the hood of Ken's broken-down VW and barks fiercely. Brenda starts walking up the street and as Ken pulls away, the dog goes flying off the top. He follows Brenda in his car for a while, then gets out and starts to walk behind her, darting in between cars so Brenda can't see him. As Brenda speeds up and begins to jog, Ken runs out of breath. He holds onto the cars for support, activating all of their alarms, losing her since he's too weak to run.

Later that afternoon, Ken decides to wait outside Brenda's aerobics class. He is dressed in his detective's raincoat and hat writing in his notebook.

Brenda leaves with her friend Elaine and bumps into Ken. Brenda, wearing no makeup and sweating, is embarrassed that she doesn't look better. She tells Ken he probably doesn't remember her from the lecture and asks him about his book.

He is flattered and tells them his new book is a secret, but it will come out soon.

When they leave, Elaine comments to Brenda that she seems to be blushing and suggests maybe Ken would be someone exciting enough to take her mind off Norman.

Brenda is getting ready for tennis, Norman for work. She tells him how much better she feels since she's been getting exercise from tennis and aerobics. Brenda says she bumped into the author yesterday and how interesting he is. She asks Norman if he wants her to pick up anything for the cruise and he says he doesn't need anything because he can't afford it, since her charges came in and she must be buying out the stores. Brenda reminds Norman it was his idea for her to look better and that costs money.

Ken is in his apartment taking purchases from brown paper bags. He has rope, knives, a gun, and Mace. He plays around with the rope, tying nooses and knots. He tries to sharpen the knives in his electric can opener and accidentally sprays himself in the face with the Mace, just missing his eyes. He looks in his medicine cabinet for prescription drugs and puts them together in an aspirin bottle. He puts all of his paraphernalia into a bowling bag without removing the ball.

Ken is waiting for Brenda to come out of her house. This time, he waits on the side of the street where she lives. The doberman comes running full speed across the street and knocks Ken to the ground. Ken starts screaming just as Brenda leaves her house.

She watches as Ken, afraid to move, lies next to the growling dog. Brenda runs over and tells the dog to go home. It immediately obeys. As she helps Ken up she asks him why he's on their street. He tells her he's been scouting the neighborhood for a house to buy after his next book comes out. He likes the tree-lined streets, and he wants a nice quiet neighborhood where he can write.

Brenda tells him what a great street it is—his family would love it. When Ken tells her he's a bachelor, she is pleased. She invites him in for a cup of coffee and offers to take care of his cuts and bruises.

Ken accepts but says he can't stay long since he has to work. He picks up his bowling bag and enters the house with Brenda.

Once inside, Brenda makes some coffee while Ken looks at all the pictures of the family. She washes off his cuts and it is obvious that she wants him to stay. As he's leaving, his bag breaks open and the bowling ball rolls across the room and everything else falls out.

Ken, trying to cover up, tells her he needs these things to work out the murder for his next book.

Brenda helps him pick up everything and puts it in a paper bag. He thanks her again and leaves.

Ken calls Norman from a pay phone and tells him he can't do the job close to home because people may have seen him around Brenda. He suggests Norman take Brenda out of town for the weekend and no one will be suspicious if it happens away from home.

Norman gets a brainstorm and tells Ken they have a cruise planned that he doesn't want to take. He'll tell Brenda he can't leave town right now, but will join the cruise at one of the ports.

Ken says that's perfect and tells Norman to drop off a ticket in the name of Luigi Savatoni at the Chinese laundry.

Norman says he'll have to work fast as the cruise leaves in a week.

Lisa and Norman are in bed together and Lisa is annoyed with him. The telephone rings and Lisa answers it and tells the caller she can't talk, she'll get back to them later. Lisa is flustered and Norman asks her who it was. Lisa lies and tells him it was a girlfriend.

Norman doesn't believe her but drops the subject. He gets excited and tells her that next week they can spend ten uninterrupted days together because Brenda is going on a New Age cruise.

Lisa acts very cold and they have an argument. Lisa also drops the news that Ms. Patterson has decided to go ahead with the malpractice suit. Norman is depressed.

The day before the cruise Brenda is packing when Norman walks into the bedroom. He tells her the bad news, he's not going on the cruise. Brenda is crushed. He discusses some legal problems he has to take care of, but he will try to meet the ship at the next port and join her. Brenda makes him promise.

Norman and Brenda are inside the cabin of the cruise ship. Norman hugs and kisses her and says he'll be joining the boat as soon as he can. Norman blurts out that he has tried being a good husband, but he just can't go on the cruise. Norman is almost in tears and Brenda, not understanding what's come over him, tells him she'll be just fine and not to worry that he's acting like he's never going to see her again. As Norman picks up his jacket from the chair, his weekly planner falls onto the chair, but neither one of them notices.

Brenda is seated at the captain's table at dinner, as she is unescorted. The captain tells her he understands her husband couldn't make it. Brenda makes sure he knows it's a temporary situation. The other guests at the table are introduced to Brenda. One man wears a triangle on his head, saying it helps his digestion. Another swallows twenty vitamins before he eats. One couple is meditating, another explains they are on a fast for a few days. Brenda thinks these people are weird and tries to excuse herself, but the captain pulls her to the dance floor telling her a good dance will relax her.

While they're dancing, Ken stares at her from behind a potted plant, writing in his notebook. He takes a bottle of pills out of his jacket and puts a few pills into his hand, returning the bottle to his pocket. He nonchalantly walks past Brenda's table and flips the pills into the air trying to drop them into her glass, but they hit a bald-headed man on the top of his head and one drops into the cleavage of a busty woman. They both look surprised and Ken rushes off.

The captain returns Brenda to her seat and brushes her body in a suggestive way. Brenda is repulsed by his actions, so she politely excuses herself saying she's feeling seasick.

The next morning, there are several groups going on. Brenda picks the group on massage, since she's feeling nervous and up-tight without Norman. The group leader is a buxom Swedish woman who directs everyone to sit in a circle and count off by twos. She then directs the ones to find a two. After some commotion everyone has a partner.

Brenda is coupled with a dirty old man. The instructions are for the couples to choose who will be the first to give the massage. Brenda chooses to give the massage first, but she is also instructed to follow her partner's directions with her eyes closed. The exercise is to give each person the experience of being the person in control or the person being led by the other's demands.

Brenda is really getting into it until the elderly man starts directing her hands toward his genital area. Brenda opens her eyes and looks dismayed when she realizes others are doing the same thing that her partner was leading her to do. She quickly gets up and leaves the room.

Brenda is in her room, reading. She hears a noise outside her cabin. Ken is lurking at the cabin door with a knife. Brenda calls out and at the sound of her voice he pretends he is the steward and tells her breakfast will be served at eight. Brenda turns off the light and goes to sleep.

Early the next morning Brenda walks along the deck. She can't believe her eyes when she sees Ken all bundled up, typing. She comes up behind him and yells, "surprise."

Ken is startled. Brenda asks him what he's doing on the cruise, especially since it's a New Age group.

Ken tells her he's doing research for his next thriller. She looks over his shoulder but Ken hides the paper from view saying it's "confidential."

Brenda can't believe the coincidence. She asks him why she hasn't seen him before and he explains it's a big ship and he's been taking his meals in his room.

He asks her if she and her husband would join him at dinner that evening to reciprocate for her kindness and acts surprised when she says he isn't on the cruise with her. He insists she join him for dinner anyway.

Brenda arrives at dinner wearing the same dress she wore to her party, but this time she looks beautiful. Ken is waiting for her at the table and when he greets her he hands her a drink. Brenda and Ken discuss his past books, dance, and drink quite a bit. There is a lot of laughter between them and Brenda is obviously enjoying herself. Brenda tells Ken she'd better get to sleep because she has a full day planned tomorrow. Ken says he writes all day, but if Norman doesn't show up he would like to be her escort. At that moment the wine steward comes over and asks if either one of them would like more wine. He addresses Ken as Mr. Savatoni. Brenda looks at Ken questioningly and he explains he doesn't want anyone to know who he really is so he can write his book in peace.

Brenda is waltzing around her cabin. She gets dizzy and sits down on the chair. Underneath her she feels a lump and discovers Norman's datebook. She doesn't open it at first, but curiosity takes over. She sees that on a line crossed through the dates of the cruise are the letters LISA. Brenda realizes the truth—Lisa is Norman's girlfriend.

Early in the morning there is a knock at Brenda's door. It is a steward with a cablegram. She reads: "Brenda, won't make the cruise, trouble at work, sorry, see you soon, your loving husband, Norman."

Brenda is very angry, but her mood changes quickly when she decides to find Ken to tell him she will be joining him for dinner. Brenda knocks on the door of his cabin.

Ken is inside typing furiously. He cracks the door. Brenda doesn't notice the noose hanging from an overhead beam, a gun with a silencer on his bed, and the handcuffs on his desk. Brenda asks if he'd still like to join her for dinner and through the crack in the door he agrees. She wonders why he's acting so strange.

That night at dinner Brenda is more relaxed. She even lets Ken hold her hand and dance close. After dinner they decide to go for a walk for some fresh air. Brenda is standing against the railing. Ken starts to put his hands around Brenda's neck as if to choke her, but she turns around and they kiss instead. She quickly pushes Ken away and tells him they shouldn't be doing this. Ken apologizes and tells her maybe she just misses her husband. She tells Ken about the cablegram, and that Norman isn't coming. Ken smiles and tells her that he will gladly act as her escort.

Montage:

Brenda and Ken partake in many activities together.

They swim, play shuffleboard, bingo, drink, dance, and finally kiss.

It is the last night of the cruise and Brenda and Ken are embraced in each other's arms, dancing and kissing. Ken persuades Brenda to go back to his cabin. Brenda is crazy about Ken and tells him she doesn't remember when she's ever felt so good or had so much fun. The minute Brenda gets inside the cabin she walks over to Ken's typewriter. He pulls her away and throws her onto the bed. She acts a little scared since Ken has been so gentle until now. He apologizes for being rough, but says he always gets that way when he wants to make love. Brenda and Ken start kissing passionately, but having had too much to drink, both fall asleep in each other's arms with their clothes on.

It is very early in the morning and Brenda wakes before Ken. She tiptoes out of bed and starts to get dressed. She can't keep herself away from the typewriter. Lying next to it is part of Ken's manuscript. Brenda starts to read and keeps looking at Ken, hoping he won't wake up. At first she is intrigued, but as she reads the manuscript she realizes she is reading about herself. She's terrified and starts gathering her clothes. Ken wakes up, sees her about to leave, and grabs her. Brenda screams. Ken grabs her and puts his hand over her mouth.

The cruise ship is docked. Everyone gets off. Norman is waiting for Brenda, for appearance's sake. Ken passes Norman and winks at him, saying he'll meet him at Norman's office in two hours. Everyone has left the ship. Norman is still waiting. He goes over to the crew and tells them his wife didn't get off the ship and he's scared something has happened to her.

They check her cabin and tell him everything is still there. They tell him they'll search the ship. After a while, they come back and tell him they have notified the police and that they will contact him. They ask him if there was anything bothering Brenda before she left on the cruise.

Norman tells them she did seem upset that he couldn't join her on the trip, but she wasn't upset enough to do anything rash. He starts to yell Brenda's name over and over, becoming hysterical.

The captain asks him if he wants to lie down, but Norman says he needs to get back to his office. The captain, remembering Brenda, tells Norman that Brenda seemed too level headed to do something, so he's sure there is a simple explanation for everything.

Norman, crying, says he hopes so and gives the captain his phone number at the office, telling him to get in touch as soon as he finds something out.

Norman enters his office with his key and hears a noise behind the reception area. He walks through the inner door to see what it is. Standing there packing her things is Lisa. She looks startled when he walks in. Lisa tells him she is packing her things and leaving for good, because she's sick of his false promises and that she's going to work for Dr. Bob.

At the sound of his name, Norman goes into a rage. He asks how she could do this to him and he confesses that Brenda isn't coming back anymore, she fell overboard, so now we can get married.

Lisa looks up just as "Luigi" walks into the office. Norman pleads with Lisa and tells her to wait until he finishes some business with the visitor.

Norman is about to give Ken $25,000 from the safe when Brenda opens the door and enters the waiting room. Lisa sees Brenda, screams at Norman, and runs out the door. Norman acts as if he's seen a ghost.

Norman is in shock as Brenda thanks him for the $25,000. Brenda points to Ken and introduces him to Norman, who thought he was Luigi. Brenda tells him Ken's the mystery writer she told him about months ago and if it weren't for Norman he never would have been able to finish his new book. "Wanting to get rid of me was the nicest thing you ever did, but now I'm getting rid of you."

Norman tells her he doesn't know what line of bull this guy is giving her, but he loves her and he would never do anything to hurt her. Brenda tells him they won't even have to use an expensive attorney because, under the circumstances, she is sure that Norman will give her anything she wants.

Norman becomes very angry and tells her that he is the doctor in the family and he earns all the money and he's paid for everything they own. Brenda smiles and asks him what he thinks his colleagues and patients would think if they knew he tried to bump off his wife. Of course, she could always go to the DA.

Ken interrupts and thanks Norman for helping him get over his writer's block and for introducing him to Brenda. He tells Norman what a wonderful person Brenda is and that they'll both be very happy.

When Norman asks if that means they're getting married, Brenda laughs and says "What, and miss all that alimony? Not on your life." She wants the $25,000 now and will send all of his things to the office.

Norman knows he's been had and sadly opens his safe, giving them the envelope with the money. Just then the phone rings, and it's the police informing Norman they have information about Brenda's whereabouts. Norman informs them they can stop their search as she showed up at his office and is safe. He says she's coming back to the ship soon to get her things.

Brenda and Ken thank Norman for the money and they leave. Norman pulls a bottle of scotch from his drawer and starts to guzzle it. He looks around his office and, drunk, goes over to the window and opens it. He has one leg out the window when he hears the bell of his outer office and someone calling, "Hello."

A young woman appears in the doorway and when she sees Norman in the window she rushes over to him. The young woman has a nice body but a plain face and is flat chested with a too-generous backside. She tells him she's looking for Lisa who is to interview her for the office manager's job. Norman tells her Lisa isn't there, but he's Dr. Shortman and he'll be glad to interview her. He climbs back into the room and looks her over, turns her around slowly and says that with a little nip, a tuck, and a lift she'll be perfect for the job.

In a large bookstore, Ken signs autographs at the signing for his best seller, "Confessions of a Hit Man." Brenda, Ken, and Max look very happy.

FADE OUT: